# Seed to Civilization

## SECOND EDITION

D1411712

*SECOND EDITION*

# Seed to Civilization

## THE STORY OF FOOD

*Charles B. Heiser, Jr.*
*INDIANA UNIVERSITY*

*W. H. FREEMAN AND COMPANY*
*San Francisco*

*Project Editor:* Judith Wilson

*Copy Editor:* Robin Fox

*Designers:* Marie Carluccio and Sharon H. Smith

*Production Coordinator:* William Murdock

*Illustration Coordinator:* Audre Loverde

*Compositor:* Graphic Typesetting Service

*Printer and Binder:* The Maple-Vail Manufacturing Group

**Library of Congress Cataloging in Publication Data**

Heiser, Charles Bixler, 1920-
  Seed to civilization.

  Bibliography: p.
  Includes index.
  1.  Agriculture—History.  2.  Food.  3.  Food crops.
4.  Biology, Economic.  I.  Title.
S419.H44  1981     630'.9      80-24635
ISBN 0-7167-1264-4
ISBN 0-7167-1265-2 (pbk.)

2 3 4 5 6 7 8 9 10  MP  8 9 8 7 6 5 4 3 2 1

**Acknowledgements**
Pages 14, 42, 70, 172, 210, 222: Courtesy FAO
Page 32: © James Motlow/Jeroboam, Inc.
Page 126: Courtesy USDA
Page 192: Courtesy of the Wine Institute

*to Dorothy*
WHO HAS KEPT ME WELL FED

# Contents

# Preface

Many problems that confront humankind today—war, poverty, hunger, pollution, race relations—are so interrelated that it is difficult to single out one as being more important than the others. Some people, however, think that hunger is the greatest, a problem that—until recently—many people didn't even know existed in the United States. Hunger certainly ranks as one of the oldest human problems. Except for the last chapter, however, this is not a book about hunger. Rather it concerns mostly the plants and animals that stand between us and starvation. The subject can be called ethnobiology, the study of plants and animals in relation to man. Ecology, the study of organisms in relation to their environment, is another of our concerns. In this case we are the organisms, and the part of the environment of interest to us is the plants and animals that provide our food. But it would be stretching a point to say that the primary emphasis of the book is ecological, and for that reason I have refrained from jumping on the current bandwagon and putting "ecology" in the title.

Of necessity, we have always had a great interest in food. Eating is the second favorite activity of many, and for some it is the first. Those of us who are not hungry can make jokes about eating, but it is hardly a laughing matter to half of the human population. We don't know exactly how many hungry people there are in the world. Even if there were a general, accepted definition of hunger, it would still be difficult to arrive at satisfactory estimates for some parts of the world. I recall many years ago seeing a slogan in a Boy Scout manual, "eat to live, don't live to eat."* That too many people live to eat is perhaps reflected

---

*This statement may be traced to Socrates, who is reported to have said, "Bad men live that they may eat and drink, whereas good men eat and drink that they may live."

by the present emphasis on the development of low calorie foods in the United States.

In this book I begin with some consideration of the origin of agriculture and why plants and animals were domesticated. The bulk of the book is concerned with basic food plants and animals, and covers where and when they were first domesticated as well as why and how they are used. I have, however, not hesitated to stray from the principal subjects from time to time when I have felt that the digression would be of general interest to my readers. There is, for example, some mention of the uses of plants and animals for purposes other than food. The plants treated include all of the basic food crops. Sugar cane and sugar beet receive somewhat less attention than the others, for although sugar is an excellent source of calories, it is important for adding interest to our diet rather than in supplying substances necessary for health. Only one chapter is given to the discussion of animals, and attention is focused on those most important as food. As I am a botanist, some may think that I have neglected animals in favor of plants, but in defense I can point out that we get all of our carbohydrates and nearly three-fourths of our protein from plant sources. Moreover, nearly all of the food we get from animals is in turn derived from plants. After all, life depends on photosynthesis; chlorophyll has been referred to as the green blood of the earth. The last chapter concerns current and future food problems and, perhaps, some controversial topics.

Teaching courses in economic botany and in plants, animals, and civilization has given me some background for this book. Although I have conducted research into the origin and relationships of some food plants, I have never worked with the really basic ones that are my chief subjects here. Thus I can't claim to be an authority. I have traveled in Latin America and therefore do have some acquaintance with many of my subjects, although there are some of which I have no first-hand knowledge, for example, the water buffalo and yams. It is in my travels in Latin American that I have seen hungry people.

The book has been written with the general reader in mind, and no particular background in biology should be necessary for understanding most of the topics. I had once assumed that the readers of a book such as this would have an elementary knowledge of human nutrition, but, judging from recent news releases, that assumption was unjustifiable, for malnutrition is not confined to the poor and uneducated but extends to the affluent and "educated" as well. Therefore, a brief treatment of nutrition is given (Chapter 3).

Although I have not tried to include all of my sources, there is a fairly extensive list of references given at the end of the book. This is included primarily for those readers who would like to pursue any subject in greater detail. Although I expect the same plants and animals to continue to serve as our principal foods for a long time to come, our detailed knowledge concerning them will change as research makes more information available. Perhaps this is nowhere more true than in the realm of prehistory, for the next archaeological investigation may uncover new information regarding the "invention" of agriculture and the earliest domesticated plants and animals.

•   •   •

Several events have occurred that make a revision of this book desirable. The energy crisis is having a serious impact upon agriculture. A large number of new works dealing with the problems of food and hunger have appeared. For these reasons I have made major changes in my last chapter, on world hunger. Several other chapters, notably Chapters 2 and 3, have been partially rewritten or have had new sections incorporated. The coverage of plants has been expanded, and chapters on sugar and oil crops have been added.

Some people have expressed surprise that the sunflower was not included in the first edition of this book, for it is a plant to which I have devoted many years of research. The answer is simple—the sunflower was not a major world crop at that time. Now that it has become one, I have given it appropriate treatment, along with cotton in Chapter 10.

A large number of new works are included in the reference section, and many of the older titles cited in the first edition have been deleted. The books and articles given for the last chapter express a variety of opinions. The inclusion of a particular work does not necessarily mean that I agree with the viewpoint expressed.

In the first edition I stated that the next archaeological investigations could possibly change our understanding of the origins of agriculture. That statement proved prophetic, for shortly after it was written the discovery of prehistoric beans in Peru (L. Kaplan, T. F. Lynch, and C. E. Smith, Jr. *Science* 197: 76–77. 1973) made it necessary to alter concepts of the origin of agriculture in the Americas. As this revision was being completed an article appeared (F. Wendorf et al., *Science* 205: 1341–1347. 1979) that may be of equal or greater significance. A few grains of barley dated at around 15,000 to 16,000 BC have been recovered from an archaeological site near Aswan, Egypt. In size, the grains are similar to domesticated barley. If, indeed, the people had domesticated barley at that time and place, it would mean that agriculture originated far earlier than has previously been thought. It also suggests that agriculture had its origin in Egypt rather than the Near East. From a study of associated artifacts at the site, the authors maintain that ground grain was used for the next 6000 years and that it did not bring about a radical change in the pattern of living. The authors conclude that if their interpretation of the evidence is correct "the development of food production was one of the great nonevents of prehistory." If this is true it would indicate that revisions of Chapters 1 and 2 are in order.

There are many people to whom I am indebted for help with this edition, particularly my students, my wife Dorothy, Virginia Flack, and Lewis Johnson. Thanks are again due to those who supplied illustrative material.

*August 1980*                                          Charles B. Heiser, Jr.

# Seed to Civilization

## SECOND EDITION

# 1

# The origin
# of agriculture

*In the sweat of thy face thou shalt eat bread.*
Genesis 3:19

People have been on earth for some two million years. Except for a minute fraction of that time, they have been hunters of animals and gatherers of plants, strictly dependent upon nature for their food. They must, at many times during their long history as hunter-gatherers, have enjoyed full stomachs, when vegetable foods were abundant or ample game was available. Early humans certainly must have experimented with nearly all of the plant resources, thus becoming experts on which ones were good to eat. They became excellent hunters and fishermen. Contrary to earlier opinion, recent studies suggest that they didn't always have to search continually just to find enough to eat and, at times, must have had considerable leisure.

There undoubtedly were times and places, however, in which people did have to spend most of their waking hours searching for food, and hunger probably was common throughout much of the preagricultural period. Certainly there could never have been much of an opportunity for large populations to have built up, even among the successful hunter-gatherers. People probably lived in small groups, for with few exceptions a given area would provide enough food for only a few. Disease and malnutrition probably contributed to keeping populations small, and it is likely that there were also some sorts of intentional population control, such as infanticide.

Then, about 10,000 years ago, food-procuring habits began to change, and in the course of time our ancestors became food producers rather than hunter-gatherers. At first they had to supplement the food they produced with food they obtained by hunting and gathering, but gradually they became less dependent on wild food sources as their domesticated plants and animals were increased in number and improved. The cultivation of plants and the keeping of animals probably required no less effort than did hunting and gathering, but in time they gave a more dependable source of food. Having a dependable food source made it possible for larger numbers of people to live together. More mouths to feed were no longer disastrous, but rather were advantageous, for with more bodies to till and reap, food could be produced more efficiently. Although some urban centers may have developed before agriculture, food production was probably the chief stimulus for the growth of villages and eventually of cities, and with the latter came civilization.

When food production became more efficient, there was time to develop the arts and sciences. Some hunter-gatherers, as was already pointed out, must have had considerable leisure, but they never made any notable advances toward civilization. An important difference between hunter-gatherers and farmers is that the former are usually nomadic whereas the latter are sedentary. But even those preagricultural people, such as certain fishermen, who had fairly stationary living sites did not develop in civilizing ways comparable to those of farmers. Agriculture probably required a far greater discipline than did any form of food collecting. Seeds had to be planted at certain seasons, some protection had to be given to the growing plants and animals, harvests had to be reaped, stored, and divided. Thus, we might argue that it was neither leisure time nor a sendentary existence but the more rigorous demands associated with an agricultural way of life that led to great cultural changes. It has been suggested, for example, that writing may have come into existence because records were needed by agricultural administrators. Plants and animals were being changed to suit needs; living in a new relation with plants and animals was, in turn, changing the way of life.

In recent years archaeological work has greatly increased our knowledge of the beginnings of agriculture, and without doubt future achaeological work will add a great deal more information. In contrast to previous generations of archaeologists who were mostly concerned with spectacular finds—tombs and temples, the contents of which would make showy museum exhibits—recent archaeologists have take a greater interest in how people lived, what they ate, and how they managed their environment. A few charred seeds or broken bones may appear rather insignificant in a museum, but they can reveal a great deal about early human activities. As a result of recent work in archaeology, done in cooperation with scientists from many other fields, we are beginning to understand the ecology of prehistoric people in many different parts of the world.

Our knowledge of what humans ate and did thousands of years ago comes from the remains of plants and animals recovered from archaeological excavations. Unlike many tools, which were made of stone and are indestructible, foods are perishable and are preserved only where conditions are ideal. The best sites are in dry regions, often in caves, and from such sites we obtain remains to use in the reconstruction of our ancestors' diet. Other human artifacts, such as flint sickles and stone querns, or grinding wheels, may also provide clues about diet, but they leave us to speculate about what plants were being harvested and prepared, and whether these were wild or cultivated. Obviously, the record of what prehistoric people ate is very incomplete, and for many areas of the earth, significant remains have yet to be found.

Drawings of animals, particularly from the later prehistoric periods, have come down to us and sometimes (but not always, by any means) can be fairly readily identified, but it is animal bones, or even fragments of them, that provide the best clues about the animals that were closely connected with people. An expert zoologist can identify species from bones, but it is not always possible to say whether remains are from domestic or wild animals.

Plant remains comprise a variety of forms. Most are seeds or fruits, but other parts, such as flower bracts, stalks, and leaves are sometimes found. A few remarkably well-preserved seeds are recovered, looking as if they had been harvested only a year before, but most seeds are charred and broken. A skilled botanist can identify such plant remains, and it can often be determined if they are from domesticated or wild plants.

Another source of information about the ancient diet is coprolites— fossil feces. By suitable preparation they can be restored to an almost fresh condition (sometimes, it is said, including the odor). Whole seeds have been found in coprolites, but most of the food material is highly fragmented and requires lengthy, painstaking analysis for identification. Such analysis is highly significant because it tells us what was actually eaten, in what combinations, and whether it was cooked or raw.

Unfortunately, material collected at an archaeological dig is some-

A.

B.

*Figure 1–1* A. Archaeological dig at Coxcatlan cave, one of the sites in the Tehuacan Valley, Mexico, that has revealed early evidence of maize. (From D. S. Byers, ed., *The Prehistory of the Tehuacan Valley*, Vol, 1. Univ. of Texas Press, Austin, 1967. Used by permission.) *B.* Increase in size of maize between c. 5000 BC and c. AD 1500 at Tehuacan. The oldest cob is slightly less than one inch long. (From D. S. Byers, ed., *The Prehistory of the Tehuacan Valley*, Vol. 1. Univ. of Texas Press, Austin, 1967. Used by permission.)

A

B.

*Figure 1–2* *A*. Einkorn wheat from archaeological site of Nea Nikomedeia, Greece. (Courtesy of W. van Zeist.) *B*. Emmer wheat from archaeological site of Nea Nikomedeia, Greece. (Courtesy of W. van Zeist.)

times not accurately identified, as has been shown for some of the early archaeological reports from Peru. Fortunately, however, the material recovered from archaeological sites is usually preserved in museums, and future investigators can examine the material to verify or correct identifications.

With the development of radiocarbon methods of dating it became possible to date, fairly accurately, the beginnings of plant cultivation. Sometimes radiocarbon dates, for one reason or another, may be open to suspicion, but when different materials from the same site are analyzed and several dates agree, we have fair assurance that they are correct within a few hundred years.

The evidence that has accumulated over the past several years indicates that agriculture probably had its origins in the Near East*— although not necessarily, as earlier supposed, in the fertile river valleys of Mesopotamia (which were to be important centers of early civilization), but more likely in the semiarid mountainous areas nearby. Dates determined for flint sickles and grinding stones discovered in these areas indicate that before 8000 BC humans had likely become collectors of wild grain, and there is evidence that a thousand or so years later they were actually cultivating grains and keeping domesticated animals. Several sites are now known in the Near East (see Figure 1–3) that give evidence of early agriculture. One of the first sites to give such evidence was at Jarmo, in Iraq, where investigations were conducted under the direction of R. J. Braidwood. In deposits dated at 6750 BC, seeds of wheat and barley and bones of goats were found. Other evidence of cultivation, dating from approximately the same time, has been found at several other sites in the Near East. Since the plants in these sites apparently represent cultivated species, we must suppose that there was an earlier period of their incipient domestication, which may have lasted for a few hundred years or more. How long it takes a plant to become fully domesticated cannot be answered precisely and it probably varies considerably from species to species. In deposits accumulated after 6500 BC we find evidence of other plants being cultivated in the Near East and Greece, and bones of various domesticated animals become more abundant.

Other centers of agriculture developed in the Old World. Whether these developments were stimulated by knowledge of agriculture in the Near East or whether they were independent developments is not certain, but the fact that some of them were based on completely different plants from those of the Near East might support the latter view. For a long time southeastern Asia has been considered an ancient center for domesticated plants, but until recently there was no archaeological

---

*The *Near East* (see map, Figure 1.3) is the term used by archaeologists to refer to the countries of southwest Asia. The term *Middle East*, widely used in the news today, includes the Near East.

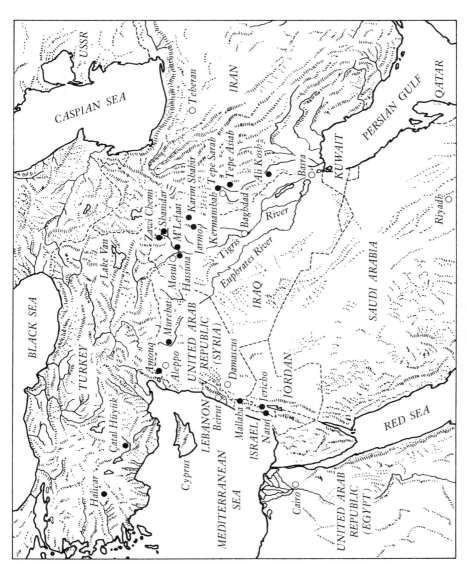

*Figure 1–3* Selected archaeological sites that show evidence of early agriculture in the Near East (solid dots).

support for this view; this is not wholly unexpected, since the climate for the most part in that area of the world is hardly conducive to preservation of food remains. In 1969, however, a report was published of an assemblage of plants from Thailand, including possibly a pea and a bean, dated at 7000 BC. As it is not definitely clear whether the plants recovered represented wild or cultivated species, we cannot yet say that agriculture was practiced as early here as it was in the Near East. We do not yet know when rice, which was to become the basic food plant of southeastern Asia, was first brought under cultivation, but it was probably considerably later than the cereals of the Near East.

In the New World, agriculture began a few thousand years later than in the Near East and had its origins in Mexico and Peru. Through a series of excavations directed by R. S. MacNeish, we now have a remarkable sequence of plants giving evidence of the period of incipient domestication in Mexico. Some indication of the earliest cultivated plants is found in the mesquite-desert regions of southwestern Tamaulipas, with gourds, squashes, beans, and chili peppers being found at levels dated as between 7000 and 5500 BC.

Following investigations at Tamaulipas, MacNeish made deliberate efforts to search for evidence of the domestication of maize, which eventually became the most important plant in the Americas. A group of caves in the arid highlands near Tehuacan in south central Mexico showed promise, and a series of excavations was begun in 1961. The results give us the best picture yet of the transitional stages leading to full-scale agriculture. Humans were probably in the Tehuacan area by 10,000 BC and for several millennia they depended on wild food sources, both plant and animal. Gradually more and more plants were cultivated, some perhaps having been domesticated at this site, others introduced from other regions. The first suggestion of cultivated plants occurs in material dated at about 5000 BC, with maize, squash, chili pepper, avocado, and amaranth being found. These plants were definitely cultivated during the next period (4900–3500 BC), together with various fruits and beans toward the end of the period. During the next thousand years other plants were added, including cotton and two new kinds of beans. The dog, which is known from historic records to have been an important food item in Mexico, is first associated with humans in the archaeological record at this time. At about the beginning of the Christian era, the inhabitants of Tehuacan had also acquired the turkey. From remains of the same period there are reports of some other plants: guava, pineapple, and peanut. The presence of these plants would be of particular interest, for the peanut is definitely South American in

*Figure 1–4* Selected New World archaeological sites that show evidence of early agriculture (solid dots).

origin and the pineapple and guava perhaps are also, which would suggest that the peoples of this area had contact with South America at this time. None of these plants has been found in any other archaeological sites in Mexico to date. A study of historical records of both peanuts and pineapple would suggest that they arrived in Mexico recently, perhaps after the coming of the Spanish.

Another early development of agriculture in the Americas occurred in Peru, perhaps even earlier than in Mexico. Two kinds of cultivated beans and a chili pepper, dated at around 6000 BC or earlier, have been recovered in a highland valley at Callejon de Huaylas in north central Peru. Previous to this discovery, archaeological plant material had been

*Figure 1–5* *A.* Hoeing and horse-drawn plow, reproduced from cave drawings in northern Italy. (Redrawn from a photograph by Emmanuel Anati.) *B.* Hoeing and ox-drawn plow, from decorations on a tomb at Beni Hasan, Egypt. (Courtesy of Egypt Exploration Society.) *C.* Present-day plowing with oxen in Egypt. (Courtesy of FAO.)

found in dry coastal sites, such as Huaca Prieta in northern Peru. Gourds, squashes, cotton, lima beans, and chili peppers are among the first plants cultivated on the coast; present evidence indicates that agriculture developed here about 2000 years later than in the highlands.

At present it is difficult to say whether agriculture in the Americas appeared first in Peru or Mexico. The fact that many of the same plants were cultivated in the two areas might suggest that agriculture spread from one of the areas to the other, but the chili peppers and the squashes of the two regions belong to different species, and it seems possible that the common bean was domesticated independently in Mexico and Peru. Thus, although the possibility remains that agriculture, or at least the idea of growing plants, diffused from one area to the other, it is just as likely that agriculture arose independently in Mexico and Peru. That there was diffusion between the two areas at a later time is clear because maize, which almost certainly had its origin in Mexico, appears in Peru by 2500–3000 BC and, as already mentioned, certain South American plants may have appeared in Mexico in pre-Columbian times.

From the foregoing account it can be seen that agriculture arose in widely separated parts of the earth, probably quite independently from place to place. But agriculture began in the Old World more than a thousand years earlier than it did in the New—could the idea of agriculture have come to the New World from the Old? The New World was peopled by immigration across the Bering Strait long before agriculture was known, and if there were subsequent crossings at this place, it was by hunters rather than agriculturists. Thus, we would have to postulate a long ocean voyage at a very early date to account for agricultural knowledge being brought to the New World. Some anthropologists have postulated that there were such voyages in prehistoric times, but much later than the time at which agriculture was established in Mexico. Therefore, it seems highly unlikely that agriculture had but a single origin. It is, in fact, likely that it had several origins in both the Old and the New World, although some people still believe that it was invented only once.

An examination of the list of food plants from all the early sites in both the New and the Old World reveals that all of the plants were propagated by seed. A large number of present-day food plants, including such important ones as the white and the sweet potato, manioc, yams, bananas, and sugar cane are propagated vegetatively—by stem cuttings, tubers, or roots—rather than from seed. Some people, notably the geographer Carl Sauer, have reasoned that cultivation of plants probably began with vegetative propagation, arguing that such cultivation is much simpler than seed planting. There is also some evidence from Old World mythology suggesting that vegetative cultivation is older than seed planting. The archaeological record, unfortunately, has not been able to provide us with clearcut answers, for many of the vegetatively cultivated plants are crops of the wet tropics, areas where the preservation of prehistoric food materials is rather unlikely. Moreover, even in dry areas, tubers and other fleshy plant parts are far less likely to be preserved than are relatively dry materials, such as seeds. While we cannot, perhaps, entirely rule out the possibility that agriculture based on vegetative propagation was earlier than seed-propagation agriculture, it seems fairly clear that it was seed planting that led to the most profound changes in our way of life. All the early high civilizations whose diets are known to us were based on seed-reproducing plants—wheat, maize, or rice—with or without accompanying animal husbandry.

Following the domestication of plants and animals, the next great advance in agriculture came with the control of water. Irrigation arose in the Near East around 5000 BC and in Mexico shortly after 1000 BC. With irrigation, considerably more food could be produced in many areas; as a result, a few people could produce enough food to feed a large population, permitting others to spend their time in pursuit of the arts and crafts and of religion. Elaborate temples, many of them standing today, were constructed by early societies that had perfected methods of irrigating their crops and testify to the amount of human labor that was made available for other pursuits.

Another important development in Old World agriculture was the use of animals to prepare the fields for planting, which was never done in the New World in prehistoric times. Along with this difference there was a basic difference in planting techniques. In the Old World the cereals (wheat, for example) were planted by broadcasting handfuls of grain, whereas in the New World the grains of maize were planted individually.

With the domestication of plants and animals there should have been a dependable food supply and, so it might be thought, hunger should have disappeared from the earth. As any intelligent person is acutely aware, however, hunger is still very much with us today. Harmony with nature has yet to be established. With the advent of agriculture, humans began changing their environment drastically. Irrigation, which initially led to greater food production, eventually destroyed some of the most fertile areas. Without adequate drainage, irrigation leads to an accumulation of salts in the soil that few plants can tolerate. That this happened in prehistoric times in the Near East is evident from archaeological findings; for barley, which is more salt tolerant than wheat, replaced the latter plant in some regions after irrigation was developed. The use of animals to till the soil led to increased areas being planted, which in time must have been accompanied by increased soil erosion. Then, along with the plants and animals that people brought under their control came others that they did not want and could not control. Rusts, smuts, and weeds soon found cultivated plants and fields a fertile territory for their development, and insects, rodents, and birds moved in to appropriate the new foods for themselves. Competition for the more fertile agricultural land led to warfare on an escalating scale, for which the powers of some of the domesticated animals were used. Hunger has always accompanied war.

Deserts now occupy many of the areas where high civilizations once flourished. Natural climatic change may in part be responsible for some of these deserts, but humankind most likely contributed through misuse of soil and water. Alteration of the environment, which began in a modest way 10,000 years ago, continues in the present on a scale never known before.

# 2

# Seeds, sex, and sacrifice

*O goddess Earth, O all-enduring wide expanses!*
*Salutation to thee.*
*Now I am going to begin cultivation.*
*Be pleased, O virtuous one.*

Ancient Sanskrit Text

The work of the archaeologist has revealed a great deal concerning the "invention" of agriculture. We now have some idea about where and when it occurred and what plants and animals were involved, but we do not know *why* plants and animals were domesticated. The answer may be very simple: It was desirable to have a dependable source of food close at hand, and what would be more obvious than to bring animals into confinement and to grow plants in some suitable place near the home? In James Michener's best-selling novel of a few years ago, *The Source*, we read that thousands of years ago the wife of Ur transplanted wild grain near her dwelling; although her first efforts failed, she eventually succeeded in bringing it under cultivation. This fictional account is of interest for two reasons. First, it postulates that planting began with woman. It seems quite possible that women deserve the credit, because they were probably responsible for the gathering of seeds and roots and the preparing of meals, and would therefore have had a much more intimate knowledge of plants than did men. Secondly, it serves to illustrate the "genius theory" of the origin of agriculture, which would have it that agriculture arose through the efforts of a single brilliant person. Most archaeologists have been unwilling to accept such a hypothesis, perhaps because it explains nothing of the circumstances leading to cultivation. This is not to say that people were any less intelligent or observant ten thousand years ago than they are today; that a seed germinates to give rise to another plant of the same kind was probably well known to those who depended on seeds as their main source of food. Knowledge of seed germination would not necessarily have led, however, to the planting of seeds. As Kent Flannery has pointed out, "a very basic problem in human culture is why cultures change their mode of subsistence at all." Our problem is to explain the change from hunting-gathering to farming. The archaeological record does not provide any definite answers.

Humans were not the world's first farmers; ants grow plants (fungi) and tend animals (aphids), and probably did so long before humankind appeared on the scene. No one has suggested, however, that people acquired their knowledge of agriculture from ants. In the past it was thought that humans naturally tend to improve themselves and that it was therefore only natural that they would turn to agriculture. Until fairly recently there has been little serious inquiry into how agriculture actually began. One of the first serious considerations of the origins of agriculture was that of V. Gordon Childe, who postulated in 1936 that a climatic change resulting in desiccation in the Near East brought people and animals together where there was water, and that this association stimulated the domestication of animals. It was Childe who proposed the term *Neolithic Revolution* for the invention of agriculture.

A widely cited hypothesis is that of Carl O. Sauer who, in 1952, advanced the idea that agriculture arose among fishermen in southeastern Asia. Fishermen, he reasoned, had a dependable food source nearby and would therefore have been more or less sedentary, giving them the time and stability to experiment with plant cultivation. He believed that as far as agriculture was concerned, necessity was not the mother of invention.

One of the first scientific studies of the origin of agriculture was that of R. J. Braidwood who, with a team of workers including biologists, carried out archaeological excavations in Iraq beginning over a quarter of a century ago. As a result of this study, Braidwood argued that there had been no major climatic change in the Near East and that food production developed " as the culmination of ever increasing cultural differentiation and specialization of human communities." He assumed that agriculture would naturally accompany familiarity with plant and animal resources.

Childe's theory of climatic change remained unsupported by evidence for some time, and some archaeologists maintained that the climate in the Near East had been relatively stable since long before agriculture began. Recently, however, evidence has been supplied that there was indeed some change in climate in the Near East, although not of the nature that Childe supposed.

In 1968, an analysis by H. E. Wright, Jr. of pollen deposits in two lake beds in Iran indicated that there was a shift in climate about 11,000 years ago. Through the analysis of fossil pollen it is possible to determine what plants grew in a given area in former times, and from this we may infer the climatic conditions under which the plants grew. The pollen analysis in Iran indicates a shift from a cover of herbaceous plants to one in which oak and pistachio trees predominated; this is interpreted as a change from a cool steppe to a warmer, and perhaps moister, savanna. Such a change would obviously have had an effect on the plants and animals present and consequently on food-procuring habits. There are no comparable pollen remains from the sites of early agriculture in the Americas, but Kent Flannery's analysis of the animal remains at Tehuacan indicates the presence of several animals before 7000 BC that were not found at later times, and this might be evidence of a climatic change. Such a change need not have been as drastic nor in the same direction as the climatic change in the Near East, but there would have been a gradual change in food resources as a result.

How else could the environment have figured? In both the Near East and Mexico the earliest known sites of agriculture are from semiarid, somewhat hilly or mountainous country. Is this simply owing to a natural bias for preservation in such settings? Evidence of agriculture is certainly far more likely to be preserved in arid or semiarid regions than in moister areas. Or is it possible that such places did favor the development of agriculture? Although this sort of environment may not seem ideal, there would have been certain advantages. These areas of diversified terrain would have provided a number of microenvironments appropriate for different species of plants and animals, which would, in turn, have offered a considerable array of wild foods and potential domesticates. Only limited travel would have been necessary to secure enough to eat, and thus communities could have been sedentary at least at certain times of the year, a necessity for the establishment of cultivation. Low rainfall, as long as it was adequate for plants at certain seasons, may have offered many advantages to early agriculturalists, in that there would have been no heavy plant cover to remove before planting, and there would likely have been fewer weeds and plant pests, both insect and fungal, than in better-watered areas. While it seems fairly evident that environment, and perhaps even climatic change, may have played a role in the origin of agriculture, it is difficult to see how these could be the sole factors or even the most important ones.

Although it has received little attention, the hypothesis advanced by Jane Jacobs in *The Economy of Cities* in 1969 deserves mention. Jacobs believes that cities gave rise to agriculture, not the reverse as is generally held. The early cities, she postulates, arose as trading centers, and agriculture actually developed in them and was later moved to outlying areas. Jacobs presents an interesting case, particularly about how animals brought to the cities for barter would have been kept alive until needed, which might have been a first step toward their domestication. She uses Çatal Hüyük, a city known to have been in existence in Turkey in 6000 BC, as evidence in support of her ideas. However, while it is becoming increasingly evident that some early cities may have originated as trading centers, the archaeological evidence available so far indicates that their basic foods were from domesticated sources, presumably in nonurban areas.

T. F. H. Allen has recently proposed certain modifications in Jacobs' model to account for the origin of plant agriculture in cities. He maintains that the sowing of seeds was known for a long time before agriculture began; however, it was seed storage bins in the early cities that provided a means of selecting seeds with particular characteristics. Thus, seed storage would have encouraged the genetic continuity necessary for the change from wild-type plants to the domesticated plants that made agriculture possible. Certainly seed storage facilities were a prerequisite to the development of agriculture, but there is evidence of storage bins in the villages of the Natufians in the Near East, before cities or agriculture developed, so it is hardly necessary to call upon the appearance of cities to explain the emergence of agriculture.

In a most ambitious attempt to solve the problem of the origin of agriculture, Charles A. Reed in 1973 assembled a group of experts from around the world, who met for several days of discussion. No consensus emerged, but the 1013-page volume resulting from the conference provides a number of provocative and stimulating articles on the subject. One of the participants in Reed's conference, Mark Cohen, later wrote his own book on the subject, in which he developed the following thesis: The only factor that can account for the irreversible and nearly uniform emergence of agriculture throughout the world is the growth of populations beyond the size which hunting and gathering would support. The events leading to the development of agriculture in various parts of the world, Cohen maintained, show a remarkable parallelism. Over 11,000 years ago, hunters and gatherers had occupied all the lands that would support their life styles, and they were forced to turn more and more to unpalatable foods. The people who started agriculture were not verging upon starvation; the population pressure was "nothing more than an imbalance between a population, its choices of food, and its work standards, which forced the population to change its eating habits or to work harder." Although agriculture did not provide a better diet, greater dietary reliability, nor greater ease in the quest for food, it did provide more calories per unit of time and per unit of space than could hunting and gathering.

Cohen is not the first to maintain that demographic pressure was responsible for the origin of agriculture, but he is the first to develop the thesis at such length. Others, including some of the participants in Reed's conference, had denied that population pressure figured in the origin of agriculture, and there is some doubt that population pressure had developed in all of the areas where Cohen thinks agriculture began—he assumes that it had four or more origins. It is also difficult to imagine that the small returns from the first attempts at cultivation would have been of much profit to people who were beginning to experience food shortages. Would they have been willing to save some seeds for planting rather than eat them all? Cohen supposes that the concept of agriculture is simple and was widely known among primitive peoples, and that all that was necessary to implement it was population pressure. But the sowing of seed and even cultivation (although not necessarily for the sake of food rewards) must be more ancient than the archaeological record has thus far revealed, and agriculture could have been implemented in different places for a variety of reasons. Perhaps population pressure was responsible for the acceptance of agriculture in some places, but it was not necessarily the primary factor everywhere.

Thus far we have assumed that the origin of agriculture was intentional. Could it have had its origin by accident, that is to say, might agriculture have been originated, not in a direct attempt to secure more food, but as a by-product of some other activity? A religious origin of agriculture was postulated in the last century, but contemporary scientists, with a few exceptions such as Erich Isaac, have not given this idea serious consideration. In order to appreciate the possible role of religion, we must make an excursion into man's beliefs concerning himself and his environment in prehistoric times.

Our knowledge of early religion is, of course, very fragmentary, and interpretations of the religious significance of material remains that have come down to us are highly speculative. It seems quite evident, however, that birth, death, and food were of fundamental importance to early humans and that concern with these affected most of their activities. As there were many mysteries connected with all of these facts of life, they became interrelated in human thought. In Paleolithic times animals, although they were killed for food, were nevertheless considered akin to man, and the seasonal cycles of the death and rebirth of vegetation were thought to be related to the human life cycle. The worship of trees and plants was probably an early manifestation of religion, and was carried down through the Neolithic period to become an important part of formal religion in early historical times. Such beliefs still survive in the folklore of many peoples. In trees and other vegetation human beings recognized a life-giving power akin to their own and to that of animals. Human fertility, that of animals, and that of vegetation were obviously closely related.

Associated with human burials from early times in many parts of Europe and Asia are small female figurines, or Venuses, made of bone, stone, or ivory. The face may be entirely lacking or crudely represented and the sexual features are often exaggerated. The well-developed abdomen on some figures is thought to represent pregnancy; figures with a prominent vulva perhaps indicate women giving birth. The rather extensive distribution of such figurines has been interpreted as evidence of a widespread mother-goddess fertility cult in Neolithic times; eventually various distinct goddesses were worshipped as regional religions developed.

Recognition of the sexual significance of the male* apparently increased during later Neolithic times, for phallic symbols from this period have been found in various regions by archaeologists. Eventually a young god—in some places considered to be a brother or son of the goddess—became a characteristic of early religions. The union of the goddess with this god was then regarded as being responsible for fertility. Among some human groups, the living king was thought to be

---

*That the female had a role in fertility, of course, could never be doubted. Exactly when the full significance of the male was recognized is not known. Some present-day primitive groups do not recognize the male's contribution to procreation, believing rather that intercourse may be necessary to allow a spirit to enter the womb or to make childbirth easier. This idea contrasts strongly with that prevalent among Western peoples during the late Middle Ages, when it was thought that the sperm contained the fully made child (the *homunculus*) and the female simply served as a house for its early development.

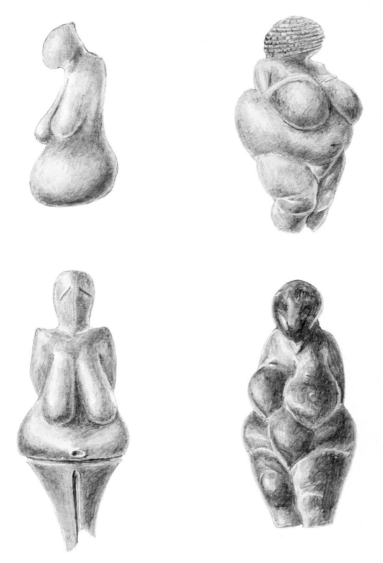

*Figure 2–1* Mother-goddess figurines from the Near East and Europe.

a god, and as such he was an important figure in sacramental marriage ceremonies relating to fertility. From this it is not difficult to see how all human sexual intercourse became symbolically associated with the fertility of plants and animals. In later times, human sexual intercourse became a part of festivals held in the fields at the time of planting to promote growth of the crops, and of other festivals associated with agriculture. The plow itself seems to have been first designed as a phallic symbol, representing man's role in bringing fertility to mother earth. Sexual offenses were thought to impair this fertility. Thus we see that in early times sex was considered to be sacred among some peoples.

With the development of agriculture, other gods joined the mother goddess and her consort to share their duties; the earth, the sky, the rain, and other natural elements were among the special domains of the various gods. In many cultures the principal male god of the pantheon (Zeus is one of the best known), who had been born of the mother goddess, eventually assumed a dominant role. The relationships among the gods became complicated and their responsibilities less clear-cut, but there were always some whose main concern was with fertility, being remnants of the earlier fertility cults. Fertility ceremonies continued during the reign of the Roman Empire, and the excesses committed at some of the festivals led the Romans to decree laws against their observance. Such ceremonies are still widely practiced among "primitive" people in many parts of the world today, and sometimes by "advanced" people as well, *although not always in a form recognized as such. Most people participating in May Day celebrations today are probably unaware that the original purpose of the festival was to promote the well being of vegetation. Other remnants of ancient practices are still found in the United States; some farmers, for example, still believe that planting should be done during certain phases of the moon and that if a menstruating woman walks through a garden the crops will fail.

The temple prostitutes mentioned in the Bible were participants in rituals derived from the earlier sacramental marriages. The prostitutes and the fertility festivals were denounced by the Israelites, who originally were pastoral desert-dwellers and not tillers of the fields. As their religion was monotheistic and their god, Jahweh (or Jehovah), was not a fertility deity, they could not view the ceremonies as legitimate religious activity or the women as anything but harlots. It has recently been pointed out that many of our present-day environmental problems may stem from the Judeo-Christian concept that the earth and every-

---

*Thomas Tryon's *Harvest Home*, a fictional account of the people of a modern day village in New England who still practice the ancient planting and harvest rites, became a best seller in 1973 and was later made into a movie for television starring Bette Davis.

thing on it were put here solely for man's use. Would things perhaps have been different if the religions of the developed nations had been derived from the fertility cults, with emphasis on reverence for mother earth and her creatures, both plant and animal?

How early sacrifice developed is not known, but there is evidence that it was practiced at Tehuacan before 5000 BC, and it became well established in most early agricultural cultures. Some people have postulated that humans were the first victims and were later replaced by animals, but it is perhaps just as likely that humans replaced animals as cultures reached a certain stage of advancement. Practically all of the domesticated animals have been used in sacrifice at one time or another, sheep, goats, and cattle all being prominent, as readers of the Old Testament are aware. No animals were more important than cattle. A cattle cult apparently was well established at Çatal Hüyük in Turkey at about 6000 BC. As part of fertility cults, cattle became associated with the gods themselves and became prominent figures in many primitive religions.

Various reasons have been advanced to explain sacrifice, the simplest being that it was to honor or appease the gods. It is likely that it was much more complicated than that, and probably sacrifice had a dual role. The human or animal being sacrificed represented the grain or the produce of the field and, at the same time, the people who were to partake of it. The sacrifice would bring about a desanctification of the plant to make it safe for humans to eat; it would also assure a future bountiful harvest of the fields. The victim in some cultures was the king. As this didn't prove to be popular with kings, in later times a lesser person was substituted. The dying king or his representative symbolized the dying vegetation, and he was replaced by a new king to represent the resurrection of vegetation and of life itself. After the abandonment of human sacrifice, effigies were sometimes used to serve the same purpose, a practice that survived until recent times in some places. That human sacrifice may not have completely disappeared, however, is evident from an account from Tanzania. In 1959, several farmers of the Wangi tribe were arrested for violation of a witchcraft ordinance. The farmers were suspected of *Wanyambuda*, an ancient tribal fertility rite in which fields were sprinkled with "medicine" made of seeds, blood, and parts of human bodies. Animal sacrifice certainly still exists; for example, among the Aymaras of highland Bolivia, llamas are still killed in special ceremonies and their blood is sprinkled on the newly planted potatoes.

Although this account of primitive religion is oversimplified and very incomplete, there can be little doubt that early religion was intimately

*Figure 2–2*   Restored cattle shrine at Çatal Hüyük, c. 6000 BC. (From James Mellaart, *Çatal Hüyük: A Neolithic Town in Anatolia.* Thames and Hudson, Limited, London, 1967. Used by permission.)

involved with the quest for food. If this is true, we might inquire if in religious beliefs we can find some clues about how domestication began.

The dog has been thought to be the first domesticated animal; dogs have served as human food in historic times and doubtless did in pre-historic times as well. In some cultures the dog may have been more important as a hunting companion than as food, and the suggestion has been made that the dog furnished great aid in bringing other animals under domestication, just as it continues to serve pastoral people today. It seems unlikely that a religious motive could have been involved in the domestication of the dog, a fuller discussion of which will be post-poned until the next chapter.

It is also entirely possible that religion had nothing whatsoever to do with the domestication of other animals. The presence of dogs may have inspired attempts at other domestications. Perhaps people brought home young animals whose mothers had been killed. The young an-imals may have been nursed by the women and become pets, leading to their domestication. This hypothesis has been considered the most likely by many authorities on the subject.

The idea that religion may have been involved, however, is not a new one. Eduard Hahn, a German geographer who published just before

*Figure 2–3* Inca sacrificing a llama. (From Poma de Ayala, c. 1600 A.D.)

the turn of the century, maintained that cattle were domesticated in order to secure animals for sacrifice at lunar fertility ceremonies. Hahn believed that cattle were chosen for such sacrifice because their crescent-shaped horns resemble the new moon. Other reasons could be suggested. The wild bull was a ferocious animal and would have inspired both fear and admiration. Perhaps men sacrificed young male animals to secure their strength and virility. That cattle became highly preferred for sacrifice and eventually even became sacred in certain cultures is quite evident, but this, of course, in itself does not necessarily mean that cattle were domesticated for religious rather than utilitarian motives.

Recent archaeological discoveries indicate that cattle were not the first ruminant animal to be domesticated, both goats and sheep being earlier. Are we to suggest that perhaps both of these animals were

*A.*

*B.*

*Figure 2–4* A. Prize cattle decorated for a festive occasion, India. (Courtesy of FAO.)
B. "Demon" guarding field of modern rice, India. Improved strains of plants and
animals exist side by side with ancient traditions and ceremonies in many parts of the
world. (Courtesy of Rockefeller Foundation.)

domesticated for religious rather than economic reasons? Certainly both
sheep and goats were widely used for sacrifice, and there is an old
Sumerian incantation referring to the sacrifice of a wild goat. If wild
animals were used for sacrifice, they had to be captured alive and kept
until the appropriate time. This could have been the first step in domestication. It is, of course, not necessary to try to account for the
domestication of all animals through religious considerations, for once
one animal had been domesticated the idea of domesticating others
certainly might have occurred to the same people, or to others who
learned of it.

Although Hahn's thesis for the origin of animal domestication has
received serious consideration by some modern authorities, the work
of Hahn's contemporary, Grant Allen, in regard to plant domestication
has been largely forgotten. Allen, a Canadian novelist, science writer,
and philosopher, speculated in a paper published in 1897 upon the
origin of seed cultivation. Reasoning that a knowledge of seed germination and the clearing of land were essential for sowing to be a success,

he looked for ways in which people might have stumbled upon these requirements; he concluded that the sowing of seeds originated as an adjunct of the primitive burial system. The observation was made, Allen believed, that plants grew exceptionally well on newly made graves. From this man would reason, not that the freshly turned and richly manured soil produced the result, but rather that the human body was responsible. Thus, there would have to be an annual sacrifice and burial to produce a good growth of plants. Allen fails to explain why intentional seeding would have occurred with the burial, and his hypothesis deserves consideration today only because he was the first to suggest a religious motive for plant agriculture.

Are there ways in which religion might have influenced seed planting other than by connection with human sacrifice? Primitive cultures must have had many rituals and ceremonies associated with both planting and harvest; and while, of course, we have no direct knowledge of these, we can make conjectures from the knowledge we have from early historical times and from primitive cultures still surviving. Prominent among these are ceremonies devoted to the "first fruits" or the "last sheaf" of the harvest, ceremonies that often imply a belief in spirits of the plants. In fact, we know from the early historical record that the harvest has not always been a joyous occasion, as might be supposed, but was formerly accompanied by much sadness and lamentation as the body of the grain spirit was reaped. As a propitiation to the spirit, people might have returned a token offering of the seeds collected, either the "first fruits" or "last sheaves". This offering could have served the same purposes as a sacrifice, removing a taboo from the plant to make it safe for mortals to eat and at the same time assuring a rich growth of the grains in the following year.

The seed offering might have been scattered over the field from which it had been gathered; examples are known of people who regarded the last sheaf as sacred and saved it for scattering over the field along with their seed in the next season. Perhaps the seed offering might actually have been buried in the soil, recognition that mother earth was the source of life. Certain Arabs are actually known to have buried a seed offering and marked the grave with stones.

Thus, we might postulate that the first seed planting was a magico-religious act to appease the gods. Such rituals, we would have to assume, took place among preagricultural seed collectors, and we can imagine the next steps. People somewhere would have recognized that the sacred sowing yielded plants. These would have been harvested in the next season, and some of the seeds would have again been returned to the gods via the soil. In time ceremonial plantings would become larger and larger, and intentional cultivation would be on its way. Sacred gardens, such as the gardens of Adonis in the Near East and Greece, were known in early times. Our knowledge of these comes from historical times, but one might ask if they antedate agriculture—stemming, perhaps, from a "first fruits" planting. Could they have originally been grown solely for religious purposes and later have served as a precursor to agriculture?

The "first fruits" and "sacred gardens" hypotheses for the origin of planting are obviously nothing more than speculation, and a number of objections can be raised to them. On the other hand, they offer a possible explanation for the rapid improvement of cultivated plants once planting was initiated. We might ask why people would save their best seeds for planting rather than eating them? Obviously, if the seeds were for the gods, they would have been the largest and most nearly perfect, or perhaps from plants showing unusual characteristics. We might postulate that artificial selection began to operate with the first offering of seeds to the spirits of the plants.

Although it seems too far-fetched to deserve much consideration, another possible explanation of the beginning of seed cultivation might be entertained: Could the origin of the planting of seeds somehow be associated with human reproduction? If the earth, as a manifestation of the mother goddess, was regarded as the womb for vegetation, perhaps there was some concept that seed would have to be planted in her, just as men plant their "seed" in women. This would mean that men would have to have had some concept of their own role in reproduction at an early date. It would hardly seem unreasonable that some people did appreciate the significance of the male in human reproduction 10,000 years ago. The historical record is too late to be of any help to us, but it may be significant that in Sumerian, the earliest written language, the word *numum* was used for both seeds of plants and the "seeds" of animals. We also find that later the Greeks used the same word for both seed and human sperm.* Some early peoples were apparently aware that a sexual union is involved in the production of fruit

---

*We know today, of course, that a seed and a sperm are not at all equivalent. A seed contains the embryo of a new plant; it develops from an ovule after there has been a union of a sperm with the egg contained within the ovule. The ovules, sometimes incorrectly called "immature seeds," or "unfertilized seeds," are found in the ovary of the flower of the higher seed plants. As the ovules develop into seeds, the ovary becomes a fruit.

*Figure 2–5* Winged guardian spirit pollinating flowers of the date palm. From an Assyrian bas-relief of the ninth century BC. Nimrud, Iraq. (Boston Museum of Fine Arts.)

and seeds. From the art work on certain early Babylonian monuments, we know that people in parts of the Near East placed clusters of flowers from male date trees in the female trees in order to secure better fruit set. Although these representations were made long after the origin of agriculture, such a sophisticated knowledge must have had much earlier antecedents. This early recognition of the role of male flowers is all the more amazing when we realize that sex in plants was not "discovered" until the end of the seventeenth century and the idea was not generally accepted until much later.*

We come to the end of our account of the origins of planting and agriculture with many questions left unanswered. Why didn't agriculture begin earlier? Certainly suitable plants and animals were available for domestication. Perhaps Braidwood is correct: human beings had to reach a certain cultural level before they were ready for agriculture. How many times did agriculture arise? Although the archaeological evidence indicates that its earliest occurrence was probably in the Near East, we are not certain about what happened in other places. If agriculture was invented more than once, were the same factors responsible in the different areas? Finally, it is apparent that we still have no completely acceptable explanation of why humankind gave up hunting and gathering for agriculture. In a recent paper Christine Niederberger has written:

> Prudent methodology leads one to exclude simple cause-and-effect mechanistic models that set forth either demographic pressure or changes in the biophysical environment† as the sole cause of the emergence of agriculture. A more fruitful approach tends to dynamic equilibrium models of adaptation that bring into play numerous natural and cultural components, in constant and complex interaction.

Perhaps we shall never be able to explain the origin of agriculture. While some may be content to ascribe it to the nameless wife of Ur or some other individual, its origins are probably complex, as Niederberger indicates. The evidence is meager, but the problem is intriguing. Perhaps future discoveries will bring us closer to the truth.

---

*The first artificial plant hybrids were made not in an attempt to improve the plants, but in an attempt to prove that sex existed in plants.

†Or religion.

# 3

# *Eating to live*

*If you do not supply nourishment equal to the nourishment departed, life will fail in vigor; and if you take away this nourishment, life is utterly destroyed.*

Leonardo Da Vinci

Human beings are, of course, omnivorous. Some people have held that before agriculture developed, meat and fish were the principal foods, and that our ancestors turned to plants only when animals became scarce. It is not certain that people have always been meat eaters, for monkeys and apes are primarily vegetarian, and very early humans may well have been too. Nevertheless, the association of broken animal bones with some early human remains suggests that the meat-eating habit was acquired very early.

The omnivorous character of our species helps explain how we acquired such a wide distribution over the earth's surface. Humans could find suitable foods almost everywhere they went. Although as a species we eat just about everything, any particular human community selects certain plants and animals for consumption. This is certainly true today, and probably extends far back into the prehistoric period. We can surmise that early man experimented at times with all of the possible food resources of his environment,* but some foods became preferred

---

*Sometimes, of course, the experiment ended in death when someone sampled too much of a poisonous plant. At other times the result may have been unexpected: certain mushrooms, for example, would have caused hallucinations. Plants causing such effects may then have been put to repeated use, either because people attached religious significance to the effects or simply because they liked them. Some plants may have been used in ways other than for food before a food use was acquired. Hemp, *Cannabis sativa*, is used for its fiber, for its edible oil, and, as marijuana, for its euphoric effect. Which of the uses was first acquired is not known.

over others. We know little of why he made the choices he did, but it has been suggested that palatability—such things as taste, texture, odor, and color—played an important role. But did these choices assure early man of all the necessary nutrients? John Yudkin answers in the affirmative: "When he ate what he liked, he ate what he needed." Obviously, had he not eaten what he needed he would have been eliminated by natural selection.

Use of fire was one of the early important cultural traits. Fire was not only a source of warmth, a means of protection from wild animals, and a tool to assist in capturing animals, but a new way to prepare food as well. Cooking has the effect of making animal protein more readily available for human use and of breaking down the starch granules of cereals so that they are more easily digested. The acquisition of fire altered eating habits. It made available foods that in the raw state were scarcely edible, or even toxic. The improved flavor that results from cooking surely must have been appreciated then as now. Use of plants for food probably increased greatly when fire came into use.

Food production also brought changes in eating habits, and new problems as well. It has been postulated that many people changed from a primarily meat diet, rich in protein, to one comprising largely cereals, which are mostly carbohydrate. If the dependence on cereals were too great, deficiency diseases could have developed, but probably most of the early agriculturists were still getting enough meat, from either wild or domesticated sources, that there was no serious problem until more recent times. However, other kinds of disease may have come with the development of agriculture. Storage of food would have brought rats, which can carry disease; and some diseases of domesticated animals, such as anthrax and brucellosis, can be transmitted directly to humans. People living in concentrated populations in newly developed urban areas would have been subject to epidemics.

Food problems are still very much with us today. Some of these, such as hunger, will be the subject of the last chapter. Some of the problems stem from the fact that many foods today are highly refined; others arise from the use of readily available or easily grown foods, such as manioc, that may have replaced more nutritious crops. It is no longer true that if one eats what he likes, he eats what he needs, for in many parts of the world today a person may eat an abundance of what he likes from the food available and not receive adequate nutrition. Life expectancy has shown a dramatic increase in the last century, and while some of this is due to improved nutrition in spite of the availability of highly refined foods, more of it is to be credited to advances in medical science.

It might be thought that most people in the United States have been exposed to the rudiments of nutrition in school. Either this is not true or they paid little attention to what they were taught, for this country has been characterized as a nation of nutritional illiterates. Malnutrition in the Third World is much publicized, but there is also malnutrition in the United States today. Only part of this results from poverty; some of it occurs among people who could buy the proper foods, but rely on the ridiculous propaganda of advertisements, diet books, and health-food "authorities." Much nonsense is written about food, and it has been estimated that 500 million dollars a year is spent on food nostrums in the United States. Apparently many people fail to realize that weight is nearly always a function of how much food goes into the body and how much is burned through exercise. As a result of poor diets, health costs in the United States run into several billion dollars a year.

Primitive people lived and reproduced without any special knowledge of nutrition (neither, of course, were they influenced by advertising propaganda), and many people today also get along well without it, but others suffer—in both the developing and the developed nations—from not having or not heeding information about nutrition.

Nutrition is the science that deals with the effects of food on the body. Unfortunately, more is known about the nutritional needs of certain domesticated animals than is known for humans, the primary reason being that animals can be studied experimentally in ways that humans cannot. The nutrients are carbohydrates, lipids, proteins, vitamins, minerals and water, the first three of which will be of primary concern here. The nutrients provide for growth and maintenance of the body's tissues and supply it with heat and energy; they also control and regulate many internal processes of the body. Both environmental and individual factors determine the amounts of nutrients needed. Obviously, someone who chops wood all day will need more calories (a calorie is a unit of energy) than someone who sits in an office; an athlete will need more than a librarian.

Carbohydrates are composed of carbon, hydrogen and oxygen. They provide about 50 percent of the calories in the United States and more than that in many other countries (Figure 3–1). A gram of carbohydrate yields four calories of energy. The complex carbohydrates include starch and cellulose. Cellulose, a major component of plants, cannot be digested by humans, but is needed for roughage. The simple carbohydrates are the sugars, such as sucrose, or table sugar, which is generally secured from either sugar cane or sugar beet, and glucose, or corn sugar. Lactose, or milk sugar, is the only sugar that comes from animals. Honey is primarily sugar and water; it contains little else of

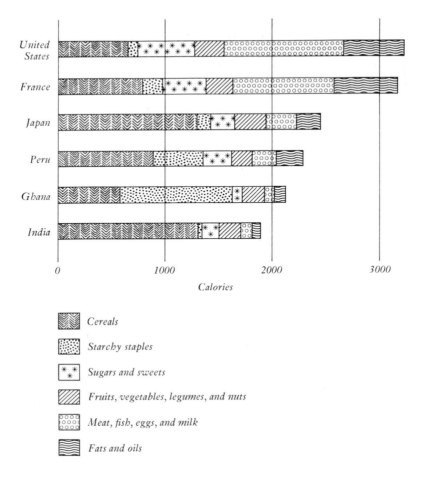

Cereals

Starchy staples

Sugars and sweets

Fruits, vegetables, legumes, and nuts

Meat, fish, eggs, and milk

Fats and oils

*Figure 3–1* Sources of food energy in selected countries. Cereals provide more than 50 percent of the calories for the world's population, but their significance varies considerably from country to country. In the more highly developed nations, animal products provide a larger proportion of calories than do the cereals. Japan is an exception. In tropical African countries, the starchy crops such as yam, manioc, and plantain furnish the greatest source of energy. The net food supply (calories) per person per day also differs greatly between the developed and the developing nations. The daily requirement of an "average" person is estimated at between 2400 and 2500 calories. (Based on data from *FAO Production Yearbook*, vol. 23, Rome, 1969.)

nutritive value, so it is little different from the other sugars in spite of the claims of some health-food faddists. Many nutritionists claim that far too much sugar—over 100 pounds per person annually—is consumed in the United States. Sugar consumption is not necessary, for the body converts starches to sugar.

Lipids, the fats and oils, are also composed of carbon, hydrogen, and oxygen, but are a much more concentrated source of energy than are carbohydrates, giving nine calories of energy per gram. The main components of the lipids are fatty acids, of which three classes are generally recognized. The saturated fatty acids are the chief constituent in animal fats but are also found in some plants; their consumption raises the level of cholesterol in the blood. The unsaturated fatty acids are found in many plants, and their consumption neither raises nor lowers the blood-cholesterol level. The polyunsaturated fatty acids, found in many plants and in fish, lower the cholesterol level in the blood. The implication of cholesterol in certain diseases such as atherosclerosis, or hardening of the arteries, has led in recent years to the increased use of plant lipids over those of animal origin, but some authorities feel that too much animal fat is still being consumed in the United States.* Some fats or oils, however, are essential in the diet, for they carry the fat-soluble vitamins.

Proteins, which differ from carbohydrates and lipids in that they contain nitrogen in addition to the other elements, are composed of amino acids. Of the twenty or so naturally occurring amino acids, eight—the so called essential amino acids—must be supplied in our food. Although the specific function of protein is to build and maintain body tissues, it is burned for energy if not enough carbohydrates and lipids are available for that purpose. Protein provides four calories of energy per gram.

Meat is most people's favorite food, and properly so in that it provides complete protein, that is, protein that includes all the essential amino acids in the proper proportions for human nutrition. Meat also supplies some vitamins and minerals. Egg is the best source of protein (Table 3–1), although some nutritionists recommend that people eat only two eggs a week because the yolk has a very high cholesterol content. Plants,

---

*In a recent report by the Food and Nutrition Board of the National Academy of Sciences it was concluded that healthy people did not need to restrict their consumption of cholesterol and fat. The report, however, was immediately criticized by a number of experts in the field of nutrition. Apparently much has yet to be learned about the role of cholesterol and fat in human nutrition.

*Table 3-1*
Essential amino acid composition (milligrams of amino acid per gram of nitrogen) of certain foods. Egg is considered to have a nearly ideal protein and the other foods are rated in comparison with egg to give a protein score. Note that protein score is not the same as protein content, which is not included in this table.

| Food | Iso-leucine | Leucine | Lysine | Methio-nine | Phenylal-anine | Threo-nine | Trypto-phan | Valine | Protein Score |
|---|---|---|---|---|---|---|---|---|---|
| Hen's egg | 393 | 551 | 436 | 210 | 358 | 320 | 93 | 428 | |
| Beef | 301 | 507 | 556 | 169 | 275 | 287 | 70 | 313 | 69 |
| Cow's milk | 295 | 596 | 487 | 157 | 336 | 278 | 88 | 362 | 60 |
| Chicken | 334 | 460 | 497 | 157 | 250 | 248 | 64 | 318 | 64 |
| Fish | 299 | 480 | 569 | 179 | 245 | 286 | 70 | 382 | 70 |
| Corn | 230 | 783 | 167 | 120 | 305 | 225 | 44 | 303 | 41 |
| Wheat | 204 | 417 | 179 | 94 | 282 | 183 | 68 | 276 | 44 |
| Rice | 238 | 514 | 237 | 145 | 322 | 244 | 78 | 344 | 57 |
| Beans | 262 | 476 | 450 | 66 | 326 | 248 | 63 | 287 | 34 |
| Soybeans | 284 | 486 | 399 | 79 | 309 | 241 | 80 | 300 | 47 |
| Potatoes | 236 | 377 | 299 | 81 | 251 | 235 | 103 | 292 | 34 |
| Manioc | 175 | 247 | 259 | 83 | 156 | 165 | 72 | 204 | 41 |
| Coconut | 244 | 419 | 220 | 120 | 283 | 212 | 68 | 339 | 55 |

SOURCE: Data from FAO Nutritional Studies, No. 24. Rome, 1970.

like all organisms, contain protein, but it is usually incomplete (for humans) in that one or more amino acids are present in insufficient amounts. The people of the world as a whole, however, get most of their protein from plants; the cereals are the chief source of both protein and carbohydrates. Meat is much more costly than plant foods, since animals themselves consume large amounts of plant materials before it is their turn to appear on the table—it takes roughly seven pounds

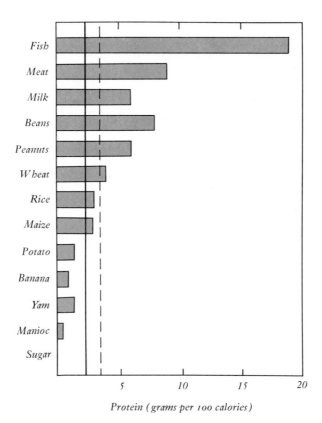

*Protein (grams per 100 calories)*

*Figure 3–2*  Protein-calorie ratios of various foods compared. It can be seen that some of the basic foods of tropical areas, such as banana, yam, and manioc are protein-poor. The approximate adult dietary requirement of protein, in grams per 100 calories of food consumed, is shown by the solid line, that for children by the dashed line.

of grain to make a pound of meat. Thus, we could feed far more people if meat eating were reduced; on the other hand, grazing animals such as cattle and sheep are able to utilize food that humans cannot. In the United States and many other developed countries, however, most of the meat-producing animals are fed grain; in fact, about three-fourths of the grain grown in this country is fed to animals. It is only in the wealthy countries that people consume large amounts of meat. In the United States the per capita consumption of meat is 164 pounds a year, in New Zealand it is 240 pounds, while in the Far East the average consumption is only a few pounds a year, although beef is increasing in importance in Japan.

There are, of course, many people who for religious or other reasons do not eat meat. They are sometimes divided into vegetarians, who eat eggs and milk products, and vegans, who do not eat any food of animal origin. The latter will not obtain enough vitamin $B_{12}$ unless they take it as a supplement, for it is found in significant quantities only in foods of animal origin. Adequate vitamin $B_{12}$ is essential for proper growth, production of red blood cells, and functioning of the central nervous system. As to protein, if plant foods are eaten in the proper combinations, a diet supplying the proper proportions of amino acids can be achieved. For example, rice is low in the amino acid lysine but high in the amino acid methionine, while beans are low in methionine but high in lysine. When eaten together, as they are in many parts of the world, rice and beans provide a fairly complete protein; so, for similar reasons, does a peanut butter sandwich. A diet limited to these foods is hardly to be recommended, however.

Many taboos have grown up concerning the eating of animals, whereas the intake of plant foods seems not to have been regulated in this way. People may think there is a rational origin for their rejection of certain foods, but most food taboos actually arose in prehistoric times and their origins will probably always remain obscure. Most taboos are associated with religion, but in no consistent way. Some religions permit the eating of sacred animals, while others forbid it. It could well be that many taboos did not have their origin in religion, but only later became associated with it. Food taboos are still very much with us. In fact, they may at times contribute to protein malnutrition of some people, who will not eat fish, eggs, or other foods because they are "unclean," or thought to be objectionable in some other way.

# 4

# *Meat: the luxury food*

*Let him not eat of either the cow or the ox; for the cow and the ox doubtless support everything here on earth. The gods spake, 'Verily, the cow and the ox support everything here: come, let us bestow on the cow and the ox whatever vigour belongs to other species!' Accordingly they bestowed on the cow and the ox whatever vigour belonged to other species; and therefore the cow and the ox eat most. Hence, were one to eat of an ox or a cow, there would be, as it were, an eating of everything, or, as it were, a going on to the end. . . . Nevertheless Yâgñavalkya said, 'I, for one, eat it, provided that it is tender.'*

Satapatha-brâhmana III, 1, 2, 21

The domestication of all of our important animal species occurred quite early. That other animals which might have been domesticated were not is probably to be partly explained as a geographic and historical accident. Most of the important domesticated animals came from the Near East, a few from southeast Asia. After they were domesticated, use of these animals spread around the world. The ancient Egyptians did keep a large number of other animals, but with the exception of the cat, none became truly domesticated. A few animals were domesticated in the New World, but with the exception of the turkey they did not become widely used outside of their homeland. Columbus brought cattle and sheep with him on his second voyage, and these Old World animals soon became widespread in the Americas. People for the most part have been content to try to adapt the same animals to new habitats rather than to exploit new species, although recently there have been a few attempts to domesticate other animals, such as the musk ox. The eland, an antelope, is now said to be truly domesticated in Africa as the result of such an attempt.

A domesticated animal is one that breeds under human control. (If we accept this definition, it follows that man is not a fully domesticated species, for he has not yet succeeded in controlling his own breeding.) This definition might be quibbled over, but it should serve. An animal may be tamed, as a wild plant may be cultivated, but that does not make either of them "domesticated." Some animals whose feeding and protection have been assumed by humankind have become so completely domesticated they are no longer able to survive without human care. Other domesticated species may occasionally become feral, or wild, as the horse did in the western United States.

Present evidence indicates that plant and animal domestication began at approximately the same time in the Near East, although it has frequently been assumed that domestication of plants preceded that of animals. The earliest date known for domesticated sheep antedates those known at present for any cultivated plant. It may be that some hunters and gatherers were domesticating animals while others were concentrating their attention on plants. However, some have argued that, even if this were true, plant cultivation and village life would have to have been established before domestication of animals could have proceeded very far. Thus, the great division of farming and pastoral peoples reflected in the Old Testament story of Cain and Abel may have been a late development.

Only abut 50 or so animals have been truly domesticated, including the honey bee, the silk moth, and a few aquatic animals such as carp and trout. Only a dozen or so of the domesticated animals are of great importance and have a wide distribution. If we omit dogs and cats, for which there are no reliable estimates, we find that chickens are the most numerous domesticates, with over six billion in the world. Cattle are second and sheep third, each numbering over a billion; these are followed by pigs, with over half a billion representatives, and goats, with slightly under half a billion. The amount of meat produced by the various animals is shown in Figure 4–1.

Today, in many parts of the world, animals are still kept in ways not very different from those of the prehistoric period, but there have been radical changes in the United States and some of the other developed nations, most of them dating back only a quarter of a century or so. The small barnyard with its variety of animals is disappearing and is being replaced by large, specialized farms. There are now automatic feeding devices, and the amount and kind of food they dispense is based

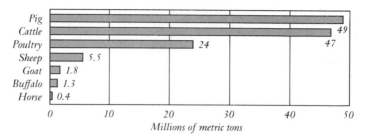

*Figure 4-1* Major meat sources for the world in 1977. Poultry includes chickens, ducks, and turkeys. (Figures from *FAO Production Yearbook*, vol. 32, Rome, 1978.)

on the latest nutritional research. Protein concentrates and feeding supplements are extensively used. Modern sanitation practices, immunizations, and treatment of diseases with antibiotics and other drugs have contributed to the production of much healthier animals.* The animals themselves have changed as a result of work done at modern breeding farms, using planned breeding systems based on extensive records and supervised by trained geneticists. Animal breeding today is based on performance characteristics such as amount and quality of milk, eggs, or meat produced, rather than on appearance as judged at state fairs or animal shows. The new developments, coupled with highly organized processing and marketing systems, have drastically changed the livestock industry in the space of a few years.

Just as they do today, animals served humankind in early times in many ways other than as food. They provided leather and wool for clothing, bones for tools, dung for fertilizer and fuel, and a means of traction and transportation; they also served for amusement and religious offerings. Today animals are also used in the manufacture of pharmaceuticals, fuel, fertilizers, greases, oil, gelatin, glue and other industrial products. Catgut, usually made from sheep intestines, is used for violin and tennis strings and sutures. Chiefly because of the existence of many synthetic products, however, we are far less dependent on

---

*But perhaps not always to healthier humans. Some scientists are contending that the increasing bacterial immunity to antibiotics used for people stems in large part from the indiscriminate use of these antibiotics in animals. Furthermore, the hormone DES (diethylstilbesterol), widely used in the United States to increase growth in steers, has been linked to cancer in humans.

animals for raw materials than were primitive peoples. Animals also serve us today as subjects in experiments for medical and scientific research.

One group of animals, the even-toed ungulates, or hoofed animals (order Artiodactyla) has provided 15 of the 22 most important domesticated animals. Of these the ruminants, or cud-chewing animals, contributed three of the most important as well as earliest domesticates: cattle, sheep, and goats. These animals, because of the microflora—bacteria and protozoans—present in their stomachs, are able to digest food that humans cannot. In a sense they were preadapted to domestication in that they were not in competition with man, being able to exist on a diet that was utterly worthless to humans. Also, the fact that they were social rather than solitary animals may have made their domestication easier. The most important food animals will be treated in greater detail in the following paragraphs. The first to be discussed, although seldom used for food today, may have first been domesticated for that purpose.

## Dogs

The dog (*Canis familiaris*)* has generally been regarded as the first domesticate, but only recently has this claim been supported by archaeology. The oldest reported remains of dogs have been found in Israel and Iraq and date from 10,000 BC. Bones dated at 8400 BC have been found in western North America. It has generally been assumed that the dog was domesticated in the Old World and came to the Americas with humans in their later migrations across the Bering Strait. It is now fairly clearly established that the wolf was the ancestor of the dog, and some have thought that earliest reported remains of dogs may in fact be of wolves. Wolves had a wide distribution in both the Old and the New World and still have a fairly extensive distribution in spite of being exterminated by man in many places. No one has yet investigated the

---

*The scientific, or species, name of a plant or animal is composed of two words: the genus name (*Canis*, in our example) and a modifying epithet (in this case, *familiaris*). Thus, *Canis familiaris* is the name of a species, or specific kind of organism, that is commonly called the dog. A genus (plural, *genera*) is composed of species that are closely related and have several characteristics in common. For example, the gray wolf (*Canis lupus*) is another species belonging to the genus *Canis*. Species may be subdivided into races, varieties, or subspecies. Genera are grouped into families, families into orders, and so on.

*Figure 4–2*   Clay dog, Colima, Mexico. Dogs for eating were fattened on maize. (Original in National Museum of Anthropology, Mexico.)

possibility that the dog in the New World could have been domesticated from indigenous wolves, rather than having come from the Old World. Wolves are easily tamed when young, and perhaps people in various places and times brought pups into their camps. The fact that dogs have certain traits in common that distinguish them from wolves does not necessarily mean that they had but a single origin. Dogs have, for example, a curly or sickle-shaped tail, in contrast to the drooping tail of their wild relatives. But selection for this character would perhaps have helped people distinguish their own animals from wild ones, and the mutation or mutations that caused it could have happened more than once.

How important dogs were to hunters in early times is the subject of some dispute; some think that they played no great role. Nor is there agreement about whether dogs were important in helping round up and control the herd animals that were the next domesticates. In times when food was in short supply, dogs and humans would have been competitors. The dog is a scavenger, however, and in time this trait became appreciated; it is still the dog that helps to keep the village clean in many areas of the world. In parts of both the Near East and South America today, dogs feed largely on human feces. The dog became prized as a source of food in many cultures, and in Mexico dogs of a special breed grown for eating were castrated for fattening. In parts of China the dog is still used for food. During the Mao regime there was a conscious attempt to eliminate dogs because they competed for food with people, and as a pet the dog largely disappeared from China. Apparently there are still plenty of dogs in China, however, as is attested by the following article which appeared in The Times (London) of January 3, 1980.

> Peking, Jan. 3—A restaurant in Jilin, north-east China, was praised by the *People's Daily* for capitalist-style enterprise in ensuring supplies of its most popular item—dog meat.
> It appealed to people to bring in their own dogs to be eaten and it would buy them. The result: in under a month, it bought 1,369 dogs—a year's supply.—UPI.

The dog became the most widely distributed domesticated animal because it was appreciated and respected as an aid in hunting, in keeping the flocks, and as a scavenger, as well as being used occasionally as a draft animal or as a source of fur or food. Although in some parts of the world the dog still earns its keep in these various ways, its role is coming more and more to be that of man's favorite pet. As such, dogs' food consumption and their contribution to pollution in large cities such as New York have been newsworthy in recent years. It has been estimated that nearly two billion dollars a year is spent on canned or packaged dog and cat food in the United States, and it has been pointed out that pets in the United States are better fed than people in some parts of the world. The Chinese perhaps had the right idea; the elimination of pets might contribute toward the eradication of hunger. Dog owners are unlikely to find this acceptable, and they might justify their position by claiming that the need for psychiatric help would increase greatly if pets were prohibited.

## Sheep

The ruminants of the family Bovideae include sheep, goats, cattle, and the water buffalo—animals valued highly not only for meat, but also for their milk and for their skins or wool. Sheep (*Ovis aries*) are the first of these animals to appear as domesticates in the archaeological record, being represented by remains from 9000 BC.

At one time wild sheep, known as urials and mouflons, were widespread across most of Asia, and exactly which race or races provided stock for the origin of the domestic forms remains somewhat speculative. The bighorn sheep (*Ovis canadensis*) of North America was never

*Figure 4–3*  Sheep in Bolivian highlands. (Courtesy of FAO.)

*Figure 4–4*  Fat-tailed sheep with cart for carrying tail, from Rudolf the Elder's *New History of Ethiopia*, AD 1682. (From Frederick E. Zeuner, *A History of Domesticated Animals.* Hutchinson, London, 1963. Used by permission.)

domesticated. Today most of the wild sheep of the Old World are mountain animals, although they probably existed in lower regions in earlier times. Most of the bones uncovered come from the Near East, and it is not always clear whether the bones found in the earliest archaeological deposits are from domesticated or wild animals. With domestication came changes in the ear, the face, the horns (which in some races disappeared entirely), the color and other characteristics of the wool, and the tail—mostly traits of little help to the archaeologist in distinguishing the bones of wild and domestic forms. A large tail with an abundance of fat was much appreciated by early people, and apparently there was deliberate selection for this character. Some sheep developed tails so heavy that carts were constructed to help them carry these appendages around. Fat-rumped sheep were also selected in early times, as animal oils were highly valued for use in lamps. Wool may have been made into felt cloth long before it was spun and woven; perhaps the spinning and weaving of wool was first done in places where such plant fibers as flax were not available. Sheep are unique among domestic animals in their adaptation to environments that are extremely unfavorable for other animal species. They probably became more widespread than goats in early times because they could survive better in hot climates. They have a panting mechanism that allows them to tolerate heat, and surprisingly, their wool may also function as a cooling device in sunny desert areas, although most authorities consider it only an adaptation for cold.

Today, as is true for nearly all of our domesticated animals, there are numerous breeds of sheep; some are specialized as producers of wool, others for meat, and still others for milk. Most breeds of sheep in the United States, however, are used for both wool and meat. Cattlemen are often opposed to sheep production because the grazing habits of sheep can destroy the rangeland and their fine hooves tend to ruin the watering places. The use of wool has declined in recent years as synthetic fibers have become widely available. Synthetic fibers are manufactured from petroleum, however, and as the price of petroleum increases, wool may again be in greater demand. Few products are the equal of wool for making clothing.

## Goats

Although dated remains of the first known domesticated sheep are 1500 years older than those of goats, this does not necessarily indicate that the goat (*Capra hircus*) was domesticated later. In many deposits bones

*Figure 4–5*  An Angora buck. (Courtesy of *Sheep and Goat Raiser.*)

are present that could have belonged to either goats or sheep; positive identification is not always a simple matter. In many places where remains of both animals are found in the same deposits, the goat remains appear earlier than those of the sheep. Wild goats, or bezoars, the now quite rare ancestral form, once extended across southern Asia from India to Crete. The original domestication could have been in the Near East, both Persia and Palestine having been suggested. The goat, in contrast to the other domesticated animals, is a browser, even at times climbing trees to get at leaves, and it can survive in areas where the food supply is inadequate for other animals. It also is able to graze and may eat grass so close to the roots as to promote erosion in seasonally dry areas. There is some controversy, however, about how detrimental the goat is to the land. Although goats have been generally condemned for their destructive grazing habits, they also have their defenders, who point out that goats are often put to pasture where cattle have already grazed and thus at times may be blamed for erosion actually started by the cattle. It has been pointed out, moreover, that shrubs may invade and ruin grasslands overgrazed by cattle, whereas goats protect such grasslands by eating shrubs.

Domesticated goats spread rapidly but were nearly always less appreciated than either sheep, which are far superior for wool production, or cattle, which are superior for milk production. In addition, both sheep and cattle were generally preferred over goats for meat. Goat production is not very significant today, except in certain steppe and mountainous areas and in some parts of Africa and Asia where goats are still more important than sheep. At present nearly half of the world's goats are found in Africa. One breed, the Angora goat, is still important for its wool, which is called mohair. Goat's milk, which in some ways is more similar to human milk than is the cow's, still has some use. The fat globules are small in size and more easily digested than those of cow's milk. It is rather difficult, however, to imagine people who had either sheep or cattle domesticating goats, which might perhaps argue for goats being the first ruminants to be domesticated, or for their being domesticated in areas somewhat removed from centers of sheep and cattle domestication.

## Cattle

Generally considered the aristocrats of the domesticated animals, cattle (*Bos taurus*), so far as we know today, were domesticated later than sheep and goats. Cattle first appear in the archaeological record shortly after the first appearance of goats, but they do not become common until much later. Whether success with other animals inspired attempts at domestication of cattle or whether they were domesticated by people unacquainted with other domesticated animals is not known. The aurochs, or wild cattle, were worshipped long before their domestication, and a religious motive for their domestication has been postulated, as was mentioned in a previous chapter. These animals had, of course, been hunted in earlier times, as some magnificent cave drawings in Europe attest. The aurochs, the last of which were killed in Poland around AD 1630, were magnificent animals. Cattle thought to be similar to some of these original wild ones have been developed in modern times in Germany by the interbreeding of modern types with certain presumably primitive characteristics. The animals ultimately produced were large, strong, temperamental, and ferocious, but quite agile, unlike the thickset beasts most common today. The domestication of the aurochs was certainly not a simple matter. One of the changes frequently accompanying domestication in animals is a decrease in size from that of the progenitor. In cattle this may well have resulted from

*Figure 4–6*  The aurochs, based on a drawing of the last surviving specimen. (From Frederick E. Zeuner, *A History of Domesticated Animals*. Hutchinson, London, 1963. Used by permission.)

an intentional selection of smaller beasts that could be more easily managed. However, it could also simply be due to an environmental factor, in that the animals may not have fed as well under domestication as they had in their natural environment.

The aurochs were widely distributed throughout the temperate parts of Europe, Asia, and North Africa. The earliest known remains of domesticated cattle, dated at 6300 BC, come from Greece, and they are known from Anatolia at 5800 BC. It seems probable that there was an independent domestication of cattle in India that gave rise to the humped types, considered a separate species (*Bos indicus*) by some zoologists. Humped cattle were present in Mesopotamia at about 4500 BC, which, if an Indian origin is accepted, implies early contacts between Mesopotamia and southeastern Asia. Crosses between the two types of cattle occurred then, as they do now. Various breeds developed quite early. As cattle were introduced into new areas there was probably mating of the cows with wild bulls, either naturally or by human design. Primitive people are thought to have staked out female animals, a practice still followed with reindeer, to entice male animals; these are then captured or killed for food. The introduction of genes from the mating of wild bulls with domesticated stock probably contributed to the early development of considerable diversity in cattle and was the foundation of new breeds.

We do not know when it was first discovered that castration could have a profound effect on the bull,* rendering it docile and manageable. A religious origin as a sacrifice of the male element, among people who worshipped cattle, has been suggested, but it is perhaps more likely that it was a purely practical matter. Cattle raisers would have found that keeping more than one bull in a herd created difficulties that could be solved by castrating all but one of them. The ox, a castrated male used for work, was one of the first beasts of burden and is still very important in parts of the Old World and Latin America. It made possible the plowing of fields after the plow came into use, perhaps around 3000 BC, and thus had a profound effect on the development of agriculture by considerably extending the area that could be tilled.

People must have used milk for food soon after the herd animals were domesticated. Although milk is regarded in some parts of the world as one of the best foods, there are many adults who cannot tolerate it, as was learned when the United States sent powdered milk as part of relief shipments to various countries. Lactose, or milk sugar, to be digested, must be broken down into simpler sugars by an enzyme called lactase. Virtually all babies produce lactase, which enables them to digest their mothers' milk. In the past it was thought that humans lose the ability to digest lactose if they are not continually fed milk after weaning, but it has recently been pointed out that there may be a genetic difference among people for retaining this ability. It is largely adults of the nondairying cultures of Africa and eastern Asia and of American Indian groups who are unable to digest lactose. These people can, however, eat fermented milk products such as yogurt and cheese, which have a lower lactose content.

In parts of Africa where they became a symbol of wealth, cattle were used for currency, and the bride price is still frequently paid with

---

*Man also quite early practiced castration on other animals, including himself. The most widely practiced method, now as then, is to open the scrotum with a knife and remove the testicles, but some people castrated their animals by pounding the testicles between stones. In addition to changing the metabolism and behavior of the male animals, castration obviously was a method of birth control. There were probably good reasons at times to restrict the breeding of animals, such as the fact that young born at certain times of the year in adverse environments might have little chance of survival. Other methods of birth control included fitting leather aprons to the animals or binding their prepuces with string. Both of these methods are still used with rams in Africa.

cattle. In some areas of Africa, cattle are seldom or never eaten, although their blood and milk may be used for human food. Members of the Masai tribe obtain blood by shooting an arrow at close range into the vein on the neck of an animal, then collecting the blood in a gourd. The Abahima of Uganda have selected their cattle for large horns, which may reach weights of 150 pounds, and a hump so large that it droops over to one side. The appearance of these animals is pleasing to the Abahima, but the large horns and humps represent no economic benefit and, in fact, may be detrimental to the well-being of the cattle.

The role of cattle in India has received considerable publicity. Cattle are sacred among the Hindus, and it has been said that they would rather die of starvation than kill their animals. This failure to use cattle as a source of food has been much criticized by outsiders. The origin of the Hindu taboo on eating cattle is obscure. That the animal was sacred may or may not have much to do with it, for some peoples do eat the animals they hold sacred. It has been suggested that the animals were so valuable as a source of traction and in providing milk that there was an early prohibition on killing them. Later, of course, the taboo may have been reinforced by the entry of cattle-eating foreigners, first the Moslems and later the British. India is overpopulated with cattle; nearly one-sixth of the world's cattle are found there, many freely roaming the streets. The animals do make many contributions: the cows provide milk, the bullocks are the principal source of traction, and the dung is used as fuel for cooking and as construction plaster. It has been pointed out, however, that in India fifteen cows are needed to produce as much milk as does one in the United States and that the Indians cannot get efficient labor from their ill-fed bullocks. Many people feel that the Indians would be far better off with fewer, more productive animals. Marvin Harris, however, points out that cattle are no more sacred in India than is the automobile in the United States, and he claims that there is a sound ecological basis for their status in India. Indian cattle are scavengers and do not compete with humans for food, and in terms of energy, India makes better use of cattle than does the United States. Certain lower class Hindus, the "untouchables," do eat the meat and also take the hides. The subject of cattle is still a highly emotional issue in India.

The Indian cattle, or zebu, sometimes known as Brahman cattle in the United States differ from other cattle in several respects. In addition to having humps, they have long heads, drooping ears, loose skin, and longer legs; they are well adapted to hot climatic zones that have a

*Figure 4–7* A zebu. These Asian cattle, which have been found superior to other cattle in many tropical and subtropical areas, have been widely used for breeding purposes. (Courtesy of FAO.)

pronounced dry season. Zebus have been extensively used in this century for breeding purposes in the southern United States and in Latin America to provide more productive cattle for these areas.

The value attached to cattle as food has led to their introduction into many parts of the world where they are not well adapted, for example, the semiarid scrub region of the western United States. Cattle cannot be grown in some parts of Africa because of parasites, chiefly tsetse flies. Various diseases still plague cattle in other parts of the world, of which hoof-and-mouth disease is one of the most serious. An outbreak of this occurred in England in 1967, and more than 400,000 cattle had to be destroyed and burned, representing a loss of $250,000,000.

Most cattle in the United States today are bred either for milk or for beef, with only 15 percent being dual purpose. Improved breeding and feeding practices and modern transportation have made cattle far more efficient meat producers than in the past, but beef still ranks as the most expensive meat in terms of the cost of feeding the animals. There have also been great advances in dairy science in recent years; milking machines, for example, are now widely used, and artificial insemination and the freezing of semen are extensively employed in breeding. High butterfat yield, once considered very important, is no longer emphasized because of the present concern over calorie and cholesterol intake and because a large number of plant oils are available as butter substitutes. In addition to cattle, the genus *Bos* has supplied three other domesticates in Asia; the mithan (*Bos frontalis*), Bali cattle (*Bos javanicus*), and the yak (*Bos grunniens*).

## Beefalo

In recent years the beefalo has received considerable promotion in the United States. This animal, originally known as cattalo, is a hybrid between cattle and the American "buffalo", or bison (*Bison bison*) another member of the bovid family; it has been known since the latter part of the last century. It was found that the bison had to serve as the female parent, for when the domestic cow was used, the broad shoulders of the calf, inherited from the bison, made birth difficult, often killing the mother. Some problems of sterility in the hybrids were encountered, but most of these seem to have been overcome. The animals raised for the market result from backcrossing the hybrids to cows. Claims have been made that beefalo are superior to cattle in a number of respects, including faster growth, a higher percentage of protein, a greater ability to withstand temperature extremes, and resistance to many diseases that affect cattle; some have disputed these claims, however. So far beefalo have made little impact on meat supplies in the United States, but of course, they may contribute more substantially in the future. These animals, however, are unlikely to be the solution to feeding a hungry world, as some of their proponents have claimed.

## Buffalo

Also a member of the bovid family—the Indian, or water, buffalo (*Bubalus bubalus*)—is still extremely important in many parts of the world. The other buffalos and bisons of Europe, North America, and Africa were never domesticated. We know little more about the domestication of the water buffalo than that it occurred in southeastern

*Figure 4–8* A dairy herd of buffalo near Calcutta. The buffalo must spend considerable time in water. (Courtesy of FAO.)

Asia, presumably sometime before 2500 BC. This buffalo thrives in tropical lowlands, likes to wallow in water, and lives largely on aquatic or semiaquatic grasses and other vegetation. Thus it is adapted to areas and foods that will not support cattle, which may explain why it is still so important today. Its use is similar to that of cattle, and it gives more milk than most breeds of cattle, with an eight percent butterfat content, twice that of cow's milk. Today the buffalo produces about half of India's milk supply. Butter made from buffalo milk is greenish-white in color; it is more solid than cow's butter and turns rancid less readily. Buffalo meat has a flavor very similar to that of beef, but it has a distinct

*Figure 4–9*   Buffalo plowing a paddy field in Burma. (Courtesy of FAO.)

bluish tinge and fat that is white. Thus far there has been little scientific effort to improve the animal.

The water buffalo spread throughout most of southeastern Asia, where it became important in preparing fields for growing rice. It is, in fact, the only animal well adapted to work in muddy fields. The late arrival of the animal in Africa and Europe is rather puzzling; it didn't reach Italy, where today its milk is used in making mozzarella cheese until about 700 AD. It is also raised in Romania, Bulgaria, and Egypt today. The water buffalo was brought to Brazil in 1903, where it has become important in the lower Amazon valley. Efforts to introduce it in many parts of Africa have failed. The animals have escaped in northern Australia and become feral, as also has happened in Brazil and in their homeland.

There are sometimes reports of hybrids between water buffalo and cattle, but these have not been scientifically verified. On the other hand, hybrids between different species of cattle (*Bos*) are not uncommon in Asia.

Horses

Most readers of this book will never have eaten horse meat, or at least, not knowingly so. Occasional "scandals" have stirred in the past when it has been found that horse meat was substituted for beef. There is nothing wrong with horse meat: wild horses were common game for our Paleolithic ancestors, and horse meat is still eaten by many people today in central Asia, the area where the horse (*Equus caballus*) was domesticated. The milk of the horse is employed for making kumiss and other fermented beverages. Why, then, do so many people refuse to eat horse flesh? As with all food taboos, the origin of this avoidance is obscure, and there probably is no logical reason. Various suggestions have been put forward. The horse, more than any other animal except dogs and cats, was man's friend and close companion, and man doesn't usually eat his close friends. Perhaps the animal was so useful in other ways—in agricultural work and transportation, or in warfare—that its eating was discouraged. Possibly Christianity played a role in the rejection of horse meat in Europe, since the eating of it was associated with pagans. There were attempts to popularize horse meat in Europe in the last century, but they largely failed except in France. In 1969 quite an outcry was raised in England when the people learned that retired horses from the Queen's pound were being sold in France for use as food. As a result the Government changed its policy, promising to put retired horses out to pasture. It seems unlikely that more widespread use of horse meat would do much to ease hunger in the world since horses, like cattle, are expensive eaters.

There is little archaeological evidence providing clues about the time and place of the domestication of the horse, but it is thought to have occurred in the steppe area of the southern Russian Turkestan region. The tarpan, a wild horse that became extinct in the last century, was probably the wild progenitor of the domestic horse. Though the domestication of the horse brought many benefits, it had some unfortunate consequences as well. Domestication had probably occurred by 3000 BC, and once they were provided with riding horses the nomadic peoples became a great scourge to the sedentary farmers. From 2000 BC on, mounted warriors and horse-drawn chariots "swept across the western world," as Zeuner expresses it. The horse made it possible for the Huns to build their great empire, and it promoted the many martial successes of the Arabs. It was later responsible for the Mongol conquests under Genghis Khan, and it helped the Spanish to conquer the Americas with great rapidity. Some American Indians rapidly adopted the horse

*Figure 4–10*  Donkeys used to haul grain. From an Egyptian tomb, c. 2400 BC. (From Charles Singer et al., eds., *History of Technology*, Vol. I. Oxford University Press, London, 1954.)

after its introduction by the Spanish, and it became important to them in hunting and warfare. Until this century the horse continued to occupy a major role in war. Two other late domesticates, the camel and the elephant, were also used in warfare, but neither was ever as important as the horse.

One other species of *Equus*, the ass, or donkey, was also domesticated, but it never became as closely associated with man as did the horse. The mule, which results from the mating of a mare and an ass,* was to become the first documented interspecific (between species) hybrid on record. The mule has been described as "an animal without pride of ancestry nor hope of descendants," which isn't quite true, for there are a few records of mules producing offspring. Throughout history the mule has been cursed for its disposition but praised for its sure-footedness, and it has made its contributions to agriculture.

In 1950 it was estimated that 86 percent of the draft power for the world's agriculture, and 25 percent for the United States, was provided by animals. The estimate for the United States seems too high, and of course, the use of animals for draft power has drastically declined in this country since that time, although for the world as a whole it is decreasing much more slowly. In 1918 there were 27 million horses in the United States. This figure declined to 3 million in 1960, at which time the census of horses was discontinued. The total number of horses,

*The reciprocal hybrid, from the mating of an ass with a stallion, is called a hinny.

however, is now thought to be somewhat higher than in 1960, for although their use in agriculture declines every year, their use in recreation and sport is on the increase. The horses don't always come cheap. In recent years there have been reports of race horses that have sold for more than a million dollars.


## Pigs

Pigs (*Sus scrofa*), like dogs, are scavengers, and hence were in more direct competition with humans for food than were the grazing animals. Also, unlike many of our other domesticated animals, the pig does not have an important dual role, being kept almost solely as a meat producer. The prolific pig was, and still is, a wonderful supplier of meat, the most productive of food per unit area of the larger domesticated animals. Although beef may be the preferred meat, more pork than beef is eaten in the United States today, probably because it is less expensive. It has been said that in the modern meat industry every part of the pig is used except the squeal. Its hide, of course, has long been appreciated, and "pig-skin" is synonymous with football in the United States. The scavenging habit of the pig may have been important among primitive people in preparing the land for farming, and in fact, pigs probably helped open the forests of Europe for crop planting. The ancient Egyptians employed pigs or sheep to tread seed into the ground during planting. At times pigs have been used for traction. One of their most interesting specialized uses is in France, where pigs, like dogs, have been trained to hunt for truffles, and it has even been reported that pigs have been used for retrieving game.

Wild pigs are native from Europe to eastern Asia, and it appears that there have been at least two separate domestications, the European pig and the Chinese pig having come from different races of the same species. Again it appears that the earliest domestication may have been in the Near East, for pig remains dated at about 7000 BC are known from Turkey. There may have been many local domestications of pigs in different parts of Europe, for they probably were not particularly difficult animals to bring into domestication. The domestication of the pig thus is somewhat later than that of the sheep. This may be due to the fact that pigs couldn't have been domesticated until there were well-established villages, since the pig is primarily a household animal, not a herd animal. The fact that it could not readily be herded may have led to the development of taboos against the pig among nomadic peoples

*Figure 4–11* Sheep used to tread in seed. The sower (right) offers grain to the animals to keep them following him. From an Egyptian tomb, c. 2400 BC. (From Charles Singer et al., eds., *History of Technology*, Vol. I. Oxford University Press, London, 1954.)

such as the Jews. To them it could have become a despised animal because it was available only to settled people, who were at the same time people with alien gods. This explanation for the origin of the taboo is not proved, of course, but it seems a more reasonable one than others that have been proposed. It seems very unlikely that primitive people could have known that pork could carry trichinosis, or that they would have rejected the animal because it was a scavenger. Mohammed influenced the rejection of pork by his followers, perhaps to make a distinction between them and the Christians, who were pork eaters. The pig was the most important sacrificial animal in ancient Rome, and it is still important in religious observations in parts of southeastern Asia and the Pacific, where the tusks often have special ceremonial significance. Among some tribes of New Guinea, pigs are eaten only on ceremonial occasions.

Just as was the case with cattle in Africa and Asia, religious beliefs may impede the improvement of pigs in some parts of the world. In an attempt to improve the food supply of the people in the area of Upper Burma, agricultural agents hybridized the local black pig with a higher-yielding spotted strain. Because the hybrids were spotted, the experiment was a failure, for the local people believed that spotted pigs were unfit for human consumption.

The modern thickset pig most widely raised in North America is derived from crosses of European and Chinese breeds first made in England more than 150 years ago. The smelly pigsty is disappearing today, as large modern farms take over pork and bacon production in the United States. The widespread idea that the pig is a dirty animal is justified only for warm regions, where it wallows in mud or urine in an attempt to keep cool. In cool climates, however, the pig is one of the cleanest of animals. Corn was found to be an ideal fattener for pigs, and therefore it is no surprise that the corn belt of the north central United States is the chief area of swine production in this country. Castration, a very simple operation with pigs, is widely practiced for purposes of fattening.* Boars intended for meat are castrated a few months before slaughter in order to eliminate an undesirable odor from their meat. The breeding of pigs in recent years has produced many changes to meet consumer requirements. People want less fat than formerly, and lard is no longer in great demand.

## Chicken

Of the domestic fowl, chickens (*Gallus domesticus*) are more important than all of the others combined, and they are one of the few important domesticated animals to have come from the Far East. The chicken is derived from the jungle fowl of India, and it has been postulated that the fowl was originally domesticated to increase its availability for use in divination, rather than for food. Attempting to foretell the future by examining chicken entrails or the perforations of the thigh bone is still practiced in some parts of southeastern Asia. This is also the area where cock fighting apparently originated. Cock fighting was enjoyed in ancient Greece, and is popular today in various parts of the world.

Although India is usually regarded as the place of domestication of the chicken, there is as yet no supporting archaeological evidence. Chickens are known from China from around 2000 BC and also from Persia and Egypt at about the same time; they reached Europe a thousand or so years later. The chicken has generally been considered a post-Columbian introduction to the Americas, but the geographer George F. Carter maintains, on the basis of early literature and linguistic evidence, that it was fairly widespread there when the Spanish arrived; he has concluded that it reached the Americas from across the Pacific. However, archaeological evidence confirming the early presence of chickens in the Americas has yet to be found. In Europe the cock was early valued (and perhaps also reviled) as a time clock, and its crowing was thought to frighten away the evil spirits of the night. In

---

*The Tsembaga of New Guinea castrate all of their male pigs, which means that they have to depend upon feral males to perpetuate the race.

some areas the chicken became an erotic and fertility symbol, the former because of the cock's elaborate courtship behavior, the latter because of the hen's abundant egg laying. On the other hand, some people in Africa avoided the chicken because they believed that eating of it or the eggs would destroy their sexual functioning and fertility.

The chicken continues to serve as a dual-purpose animal in many parts of the world; in many places the birds are scrawny, largely scavenging for an existence, and producing but few eggs, which are rarely eaten by the owners but are taken to the market for sale. More and more, the production of eggs and of "broilers" are separate operations in the industrialized nations, where the raising of chickens depends on procedures that offer a striking contrast to the old barnyard methods. In fact, the broiler farm may be compared to a modern factory with its assembly lines. Mammoth incubators, automatic feeding, watering, ventilating and cleaning, and defeathering machinery are utilized in the production of fowl for the supermarket or the chicken-house chain restaurant. The breeding of poultry is more highly developed than that of any other group of animals, and hybrid chickens have come to be of great importance in recent years.

## Other Old World Domesticates

There are, of course, several other animals—camels, elephants, and reindeer, for example—that are used in the Old World. None of them, however, figured as prominently in early agriculture as did those already treated. Nor are these other animals as important for food sources today as some of those previously discussed. This is not to say, however, that some of the other domesticated animals—the rabbit, for example, which can be raised very economically—cannot make significant contributions in the future by supplying much needed protein in various parts of the world.

## New World Domesticates

In the Americas only a very few species of animals were domesticated, and none of these, with the exception of the turkey (*Meleagris gallopavo*) has even become significant outside of the New World. Wild turkeys, now rare, were once fairly widely distributed in North America and Mexico, and the turkey was a well domesticated animal in Mexico at

*Figure 4–12*  Roasted guinea pigs for sale in a market in Quito, Ecuador.

the time of the arrival of the Spanish. Whether the bird had reached South America in pre-Conquest times is not entirely clear. "Pavos", generally thought to mean turkeys, are mentioned in the early Spanish accounts of South America, but these references may actually have been to other large birds. Our name *turkey* is in a sense an error, in that the American bird was confused with the turkeycock, or peafowl, in England and the name became transferred to it.

In South America, four animals were domesticated in prehistoric times. The Muscovy duck (*Carina moschata*)—why it is called Muscovy has never been entirely satisfactorily explained—is the other fowl that came from the Americas. The guinea pig, cavy, or "cui" (*Cavia porcellus*) is a rodent now widely used as a laboratory experimental animal. It

*Figure 4–13*   Llamas in Peru. (Courtesy of FAO.)

was domesticated in the Andes and is still an important food animal among the Indians there, living in their houses with them and often appearing for sale in the markets, either alive or roasted. The name is thought to stem from its arrival in Europe from Guinea, the animal having gone first from South America to West Africa. More important than either of these species, however, are the llama (*Lama glama*) and the alpaca (*Lama pacos*), both of the camel family and probably derived from the wild guanaco. A relative of these, the vicuña, much prized for its wool, was never domesticated, although attempts are now being made to domesticate it in Peru.

Llama remains have been reported at a site of early agriculture in Peru, dated about 3000 BC; the original domestication was probably in highland Peru. Llamas played many important roles among the Andean Indians. They were used for sacrifice—pure black or white animals were preferred for this purpose—their lungs and entrails were examined for omens, and potatoes were ritually treated with their blood before planting. A religious motive for their domestication has, of course, been suggested. The animal was used as a beast of burden, for food, as a source of wool and hide, and as a source of medicine and of dung for fuel, but it was neither ridden nor milked. As a beast of burden the llama carries only a relatively small load, a little more than 100 pounds, and it travels 10 to 18 miles a day. A great advantage is that it can live off the sparse fodder provided by the Andean highlands. The alpaca, which is slightly smaller than the llama, is used for most of the same purposes, but not as a beast of burden. Its wool, however, is far superior to that of the llama.

After the arrival of the Spanish, the Old World domesticated animals spread throughout the Americas. In Peru it is sometimes said that it took three other animals to replace the llama—cattle for food, the donkey as a beast of burden, and sheep for wool—and that all of them required more food than the llama. Both the llama and the alpaca have persisted in the high Andes, where they are so well adapted, and they will probably continue to do so for some time to come. Although their range is considerably more restricted than it was at the height of the Inca empire, they are a common sight in parts of highland Peru and Bolivia, where they are still used much as in the past and are gaily decorated for ceremonial occasions.

# 5

# Grasses: the staff of life

*All flesh is grass.*
Isaiah 40:6.


Of all the various plant groups—algae, fungi, mosses, ferns, gymnosperms,* and flowering plants—the last named has furnished us with nearly all of the species we use for food and clothing and in countless other ways. Since the flowering plants, or angiosperms, comprise nearly two-thirds of all species of plants and are the dominant vegetation on the earth's land surface, their great use perhaps should not come as a surprise; but their significance derives not so much from their numbers as from the fact that they are the only plants that produce fruits and seeds. Of the 200,000 or more species of flowering plants known, only 3,000 or so have been used to any extent by humans for food. Of these about 200 have become more or less domesticated, of which some dozen or so are the primary foods that stand between us and starvation. The grasses are foremost in this regard (Figure 5–1).† Of the 300 or so families of flowering plants, none is of greater importance to us than the grass family, known scientifically as the family Gramineae.

---

*The gymnosperms, which include the conifers, such as pine, are particularly important to us for their wood.

†Quite a number of plants are sometimes called grass, including marijuana, that do not belong to the botanical family that carries this name. The true grasses are distinguished from other plants by a combination of floral and vegetative features. Their small flowers, which lack petals, are enclosed in specialized scales, or bracts. The flowers are grouped in small clusters, or spikelets, and the spikelets, in turn, are arranged in clusters, such as a head of wheat or a corn tassel.

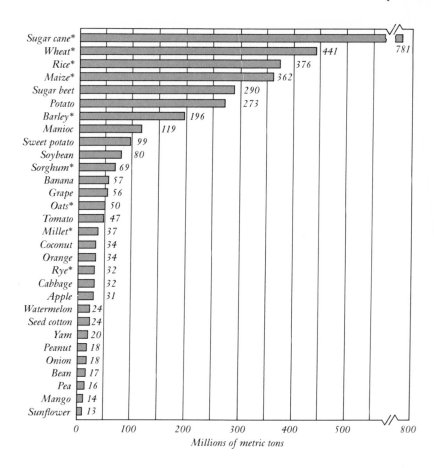

*Figure 5–1*  Production of the world's major crops in 1977. The importance of members of the grass family (indicated by an asterisk) is obvious. Considerable amounts of some of the crops listed are not used as food. Most of the yield of grapes goes into the production of wine. The water content of the material should be taken into account in evaluating the overall importance of the various crops. Sugar cane contains far more water than do the cereals, and the fleshy fruits such as tomato and watermelon are well over 90 percent water. The millets represent species belonging to several different genera and thus are not directly comparable with the other entries, which represent either a single species or several species belonging to a single genus. Plantains have been included with bananas. (Statistics from *FAO Production Yearbook*, vol. 32, Rome, 1978. The yield for yams is for 1975.)

From the time of the earliest seed collectors to the present the grasses have supplied us with one of our principal foods. Their fruits, or grains, often called seeds, each develop from the ovary of a single flower and each contains a single true seed. Inside the seed coat is a rich layer of stored food, mostly starch, known as the endosperm. This concentrated reserve food, which is designed to provide energy for the germinating embryo, is also a rich source of carbohydrates for us and other animals. The embryo, sometimes called the germ of the seed, contains protein and oil. Some vitamins and minerals are also present in the grain. Thus, the grasses come close to being the ideal source of plant food, but alone they can not sustain us very well, for their protein does not contain all the amino acids in the necessary proportions essential for human well being. The cereals are also deficient in calcium and, except for the yellow form of maize, in vitamin A, and the dried seeds do not contain vitamin C. The grains give high yields, are fairly easy to collect, and may be stored for long periods of time without spoiling. Little wonder that the cereals—so named from Ceres, the Roman goddess of crops—have become the chief crop of most people throughout the world. More than 70 percent of farm land is planted to cereals, which provide the human population with more than 50 percent of its calories.

Wheat and barley formed the basis for early civilization in the Near East; rice was the food that allowed the development of high cultures in the Far East; and maize* was responsible for the evolution of the great civilizations of the Americas. These four grasses, along with oats and rye, are the cereals best known to people of the Western world. In some parts of the world, particularly in Africa and Asia, other grasses, better adapted to climates too severe for the major cereals, are grown. The most important of these is grain sorghum. A number of different grasses, sometimes lumped under the name "millets," are also fairly extensively grown as cereals, as is Job's-tears, perhaps best known in the United States in the form of beads used for necklaces. All of the grasses thus far mentioned, with the exception of maize, are native to the Old World, and it is sometimes stated that maize was the only true cereal ever domesticated in the New World. This is not quite true, for in prehistoric times Indians in southern South America cultivated a

---

*Maize is the name of the plant that is commonly called *corn* in the United States. In other English-speaking countries, *corn* generally means the most common cereal, or sometimes any cereal. In the Bible *corn* usually refers to wheat, as it does in much of the United Kingdom today—except in Scotland, where it refers to oats.

74

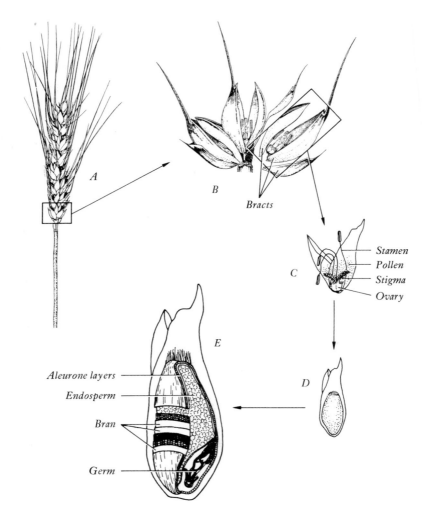

*Figure 5–2* Flowers and grain of wheat. *A.* Head, or spike, composed of many spikelets. *B.* Spikelet with three flowers. *C.* Single flower showing parts. *D.* Maturing ovary, or young grain. *E.* Mature fruit, or grain, surrounded by bracts, or chaff; dissected to show various parts. The outer layers of the grain, the bran, contain some carbohydrates, B vitamins, and minerals. The outer part of the endosperm, called the aleurone layer, contains protein and phosphorus. The endosperm, or food layer, is composed mostly of carbohydrates; this is the only part used in making highly refined flour. The germ, or embryo, is rich in fats, protein, and vitamins and contains some minerals and carbohydrates. (*A-D* from "Hybrid Wheat" by Byrd C. Curtis and David R. Johnston. Copyright © 1969 by Scientific American, Inc. All rights reserved. *E* from Wheat Flour Institute.)

*Figure 5–3*  Bamboo plants. (Courtesy of FAO.)

brome grass for its grain, and in parts of Mexico a species of panic grass was grown, but neither of these was to achieve any importance. Not all the nutrition derived from the grasses is in the form of grain—-sugar cane, a grass, is the source of 50 percent or more of the sugar produced in the world—and quite apart from their use as food, grasses serve humankind in many other ways.

With the coming of civilization, our ancestors needed something to bring relief from the worries and cares that accompanied it. For this they often turned to the same plants that had played a fundamental part in making civilization possible. Fermented beverages can be made from a great variety of plants, and before civilization appeared people had probably already discovered that certain grasses serve to make excellent beer. Barley very early came to prominence in this regard, a position it has never relinquished. Today, of course, the grasses provide major ingredients for popular alcoholic beverages—rice is necessary for the making of *sake*, maize for bourbon, and sugar cane for rum. Whether this use of grasses has been a service or disservice to humankind is the subject of divided opinions.

Tropical grasses of tremendous importance are the bamboos, exceptional in the grass family for their size and woodiness. Practically indispensable in parts of the tropical world, they are little appreciated in temperate areas, although some people may recall that they were once used for the pole vault and they are still used for fishing rods. I know of no better way to tell of the importance of the bamboos than to quote from a paper that a Thai student, Sa-korn Trinandwan, once wrote for my course in Economic Botany.

> I write this paper with gratitude and great respect for bamboo. In the poor families of the tropical people, the child is born on the floor of bamboo ribs under the bamboo roof in the bamboo hut. He is rocked in the bamboo cradle by his mother. He plays with toys which are made of bamboo. When he grows up and does something wrong, he will be punished by his mother with a bamboo rod. Sometimes he entertains himself with the bamboo flute. Sometimes he eats the bamboo shoots which are cooked on the bamboo fire. Then he grows up to be a man and makes love under the bamboo shade and builds a bamboo hut for his wife. When he grows old and dies, his body is buried in the bamboo coffin. The bamboos give sadness and happiness to the life of man from generation to generation. Bamboos are parts of men's lives. Bamboos are a part of their blood, and they seek their ways to the human soul.
>
> Bamboos can get along very well among the rich people. They get into the rich people's houses and serve them in the form of beautiful furniture. Sometimes bamboos get into their gardens and spend their entire lives with them. In the ancient times, even the king had to spend the night in the bamboo camp. During World War II, the prisoners of war spent part of their lives in the Japanese bamboo camps. How much the bamboos serve the man, whether rich or poor, high or low.

The importance of grasses for the feeding of livestock is fairly obvious. Although the saying that "all meat is grass" is not true, it comes close to being so, since the grain and the fresh or dried leaves of grasses are the principal foods of most of our domesticated animals.

Not to be overlooked is the importance of grasses as ornamentals. Although a few grasses are occasionally grown singly for their aesthetic value, the chief claim to significance of grasses as ornamentals comes in their use for lawns. With the widespread movement to suburbia in the United States in recent years, billions of dollars have been spent for blue grass seed or sod, for other lawn grasses, and for fertilizers, mowers, and so on. At the same time, a tremendous amount of money has been spent trying to eliminate undesirable plants from lawns, chief among them another member of the same family, crab grass.

*Figure 5-4* Some products of bamboo in Thailand. (Courtesy of Sa-korn Trinandwan.)

In addition to crab grass, the family furnishes us with a number of other weeds, but then, this is equally true of most large plant families. There is no good scientific definition of a weed. Weeds are plants that follow man, growing best in the areas disturbed by him or his domesticated animals. They are sometimes referred to as "unwanted plants" or as "plants whose virtues have not yet been discovered." The latter definition has more than a modicum of truth in it. Rye and oats in prehistoric times were weeds of the cultivated wheat and barley fields. They spread with the domesticated plants as the latter were brought into new areas; in northern Europe they grew better than the wheat and barley, and in time they became intentionally cultivated and eventually domesticated.

Finally, in this brief introduction to the significance of grasses, mention must be made of their importance to soil conservation. A cover of grass affords greater protection against erosion of soil than any other plant, for the blades bend to cover the ground while rain is falling, forming a mat that permits the water to run off with very little or no loss of soil. Various grasses are thus often planted in areas subject to soil erosion. Some grasses too, particularly rye, are planted to be plowed under, to improve the texture and fertility of the soil.

People have used grasses in many other ways, but rather than explore these, let us consider at greater length the grasses that have contributed the most to our food.

## Wheat

The most widely cultivated plant in the world today, wheat, as was pointed out in an earlier chapter, was one of the first two cultivated plants. The other, barley, has continued to the present day to be of importance, but chiefly as animal feed and as the source of malt for making beer. Wheat has become the principal cereal, being more widely used for the making of bread than any other cereal because of the quality and quantity of its characteristic protein, called gluten. As it is gluten that makes bread dough stick together and gives it the ability to retain gas, the higher the proportion of gluten in the flour, the better for making leavened bread.

Bread, of course, was not one of the first prepared foods, for the early wheats were hardly suited to bread making. It seems likely that wild wheat and the early cultivated wheats were prepared by parching, which would have the advantage of removing the chaffy bracts surrounding the grain as well as making it more readily digestible. By grinding the parched grain and adding water, people could make a gruel. A beer of sorts may have been another early product in which grain was used. To make beer, it would be necessary for some of the starch of the grain to be converted into sugar,* which then could be fermented by wild yeasts, unknowingly introduced along with the plant materials. Long ago, people found such a brew to their liking, and

---

*Starch is hydrolyzed to a fermentable sugar by the action of certain enzymes. Such enzymes could have been supplied in beer making by certain molds, by malting (that is, by germinating seeds), or by mastication. Malting barley is known to be quite ancient, being recorded in early written documents.

although they may not have known it, it was a nutritious drink. Yeast, in fact, may have become a cultivated plant before the grains did, for yeast-containing residues from beer made from wild ingredients might have been used for starting new batches, meaning that the yeast was actually being cultivated. Some time later, leavened bread resulted from the same process, the carbon dioxide bubbles formed during fermentation becoming trapped in the sticky dough and causing it to rise. Unleavened bread, of course, was probably used earlier and continues to have significance in certain religious ceremonies.

Wild wheats, which still are found in the Near East in some abundance, were being collected by humans long before domestication occurred. Flint blades, which were apparently used for sickles to harvest grain, have been found in archaeological deposits dating back some 12,000 years. Milling stones and querns for grinding are even older, although we do not know for certain that they were used for cereals. Evidence that the wild cereals could have supplied an abundance of food was provided by Jack Harlan, an American botanist, a few years ago. With a flint sickle he was able to harvest four pounds of wild grain in an hour. Thus, as he points out, a person equipped with such a tool could have in a space of a few weeks harvested more than enough grain to feed a family for a year.

We may never know for certain why grain became cultivated, but we do now have considerable information about how wild wheat became transformed into the most important domesticated plant. We shall see that the process, which took place in the prehistoric period, involved accidental or natural hybridizations followed by a doubling of chromosomes. The working out of the details of the origin of domesticated wheats is as fascinating as any detective story (at least to the botanist) and the understanding of the origin of these plants has furnished knowledge of great importance to plant breeders in their efforts to improve them.

Our present understanding of wheat's origins is not the work of one or a few people, but results from a great many botanical studies conducted during this century in Germany, Russia, Japan, the United States, England, and Israel. Taxonomists had described many different species of wheat during the previous 150 years, and Linnaeus had provided the genus name, choosing *Triticum*, an old Latin name for cereal. In the early part of this century, taxonomists recognized on the basis of the appearance of the plants that there were three groups of species of wheat. Shortly after, it was shown that the three different groups were characterized by different chromosome numbers, the diploids having 14 chromosomes, the tetraploids having 28, and the hexaploids 42. Thus, the wheat species form a polyploid series with a base chromosome number of seven.*

The species with 14 chromosomes include the wild einkorn (*Triticum boeoticum*), which still grows wild in the Near East, and the cultivated einkorn (*Triticum monococcum*), which differs little from its wild counterpart except in having slightly larger grains and less brittle fruit stalks that prevent the grains from falling quite so readily. Einkorn is a low-yielding species, but it is cultivated to a limited extent in the Near East and in central and southeastern Europe. The chromosome sets of the diploid wheat are designated AA, each letter representing one set of chromosomes (Figure 5–5).

The 28-chromosome, or tetraploid, wheats comprise several species. One of these, *Triticum dicoccoides*, or wild emmer, is a wild species. The cultivated emmer (*Triticum dicoccum*) is grown principally in Asia and the Mediterranean area. Formerly used for making bread and pastries, it is now used mainly for livestock feed. Both of the emmers have covered, or hulled, grains, a characteristic of wild grasses. Several of the tetraploid wheats have naked grains that thresh free, a boon to man, of course, but detrimental for a wild species. Among the species with naked grains we find durum, or macaroni, wheat (*Triticum durum*), which is one of the important wheats today. The chromosome composition of the tetraploids is designated AABB. Several hexaploid species and varieties, with 42 chromosomes, are also known. These include some with hulled grains, such as spelt (*Triticum spelta*), once the principal wheat of Europe, and some with naked grains, such as bread, or common, wheat (*Triticum aestivum*), which has become the type most widely grown throughout the world today and preferred for bread. The hexaploids are designated AABBDD.

---

*Chromosomes, found in the cells of most organisms, contain the genes that control transmission of hereditary characteristics. The eggs and sperms of an organism each contain one set of chromosomes and are called haploid. The union of sperm and egg as a result of fertilization gives rise to a plant or animal, designated as diploid, that has two sets of chromosomes, one derived from each parent. Most plants and animals are diploid, but particularly in plants, we may find individuals or species characterized by having more than two sets of chromosomes; these are known as polyploids. Polyploidy results from an "accident" in the chromosome division in a species or, more frequently, in a hybrid between species. In the wheats there are two sorts of polyploids: tetraploids having four sets of chromosomes and hexaploids having six. Chromosomes of a plant are studied by observation of dividing cells. Usually anthers in which young pollen grains are developing or young roots are used. The structures are crushed and treated with a stain that makes the chromosomes visible and then examined under a compound microscope at high magnification.

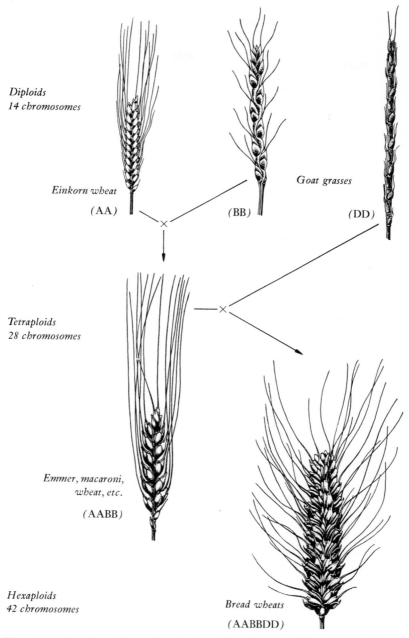

*Figure 5–5*  Evolution of domesticated wheats. (Modified from "Wheat" by Paul C. Mangelsdorf. Copyright © 1953 by Scientific American, Inc. All rights reserved.)

In a polyploid series, the most ancient species is the one with the lowest chromosome number, and from this it would follow that einkorn (AA) is the ancestor of the other wheats. Einkorn hybridized with another species with chromosome set BB and gave rise by chromosome doubling to the tetraploid, or AABB, species. One of these tetraploids, in turn, hybridized with still another species, with the DD chromosome constitution, and this triploid hybrid in turn doubled its chromosomes to give rise to the hexaploid, or AABBDD, wheats (Figure 5–5). Attempts to identify the donors of the BB and DD chromosome sets have been the subject of intensive study over the years. Both of them come from goat grasses, weedy grasses worthless to man except for their contribution of desirable chromosomes to wheat. The DD set, which contributes to the high gluten content of the hexaploids and also makes them better adapted to extreme environments than are the other wheats, comes from *Triticum tauschii*,* a species that ranges from Turkey to Kashmir and Pakistan. Although various species have been suggested, there is yet no agreement on the contributor of the BB chromosome set. It is, of course, possible that the donor species is now extinct or has changed to such an extent that it can no longer be clearly identified.

Humans apparently had no role in the development of the polyploid wheats, except perhaps for unwittingly bringing the cultivated plants and the weed together so that it was possible for hybridization to occur. In addition to the accidental hybridizations and chromosome doublings that gave rise to the tetraploid and hexaploid wheats, one other event was of paramount importance in their evolution. This was a mutation that influenced chromosome pairing in the polyploid plants so that they had good fertility. Few other single mutations have had such great importance in the development of the whole of western civilization.

Archaeological work has helped to supply approximate dates for the development of the wheat species, as well as to indicate the general areas where they developed. Wild emmer has been reported from the archaeological site of Tell Mureybat on the banks of the Euphrates, dated at about 8000 BC. Wild einkorn, einkorn, and emmer are all found at Ali Kosh in southwestern Iran in deposits dated between 7500 and 6750 BC, and both wild einkorn and emmer occur at Haçilar in west central Anatolia, dated at about 7000 BC. At Jarmo in the Iraqi Kurdistan, in deposits dated at about 6750 BC, both wild and cultivated

---

*Before their close relationship to the wheats was known, the goat grasses were placed in the genus *Aegilops*. In earlier works the name *Aegilops squarrosa* was used for *Triticum tauschii*.

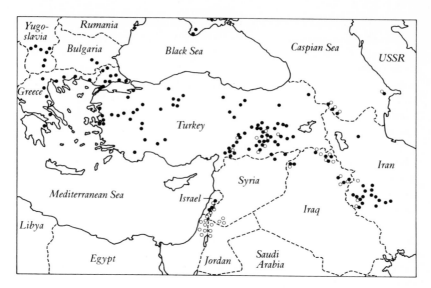

*Figure 5–6* Current distribution of wild einkorn (solid dots) and wild emmer (open circles). (Adapted from "Distribution of Wild Wheats and Barley" by Jack R. Harlan and Daniel Zohary, *Science,* 153: 1074–1080, 1960. Copyright © 1966 by the American Association for the Advancement of Science.)

einkorn have been found , along with grains that appear to be somewhat transitional between wild and cultivated emmer. Deposits in Greece dated at 6100 BC reveal both einkorn and emmer. From these finds it appears that people may still have been collecting wild wheats at the same time cultivation was beginning, which is hardly surprising since the early cultivated plants were probably neither high yielding nor extensively grown. Both einkorn and emmer appear to have come into cultivation at about the same time, with emmer being the more widely cultivated. The hexaploid wheats appear surprisingly early, for there is evidence for one of them, club wheat, in Syria around 7000 BC. Early appearances of bread wheat are found at Çatal Hüyük in Anatolia in the period 5850–5600 BC, at Tepe Sabz in southwestern Iran between 5500 and 5000 BC, and at Haçilar between 5800 and 5000 BC. A tentative identification would place the species in Greece at about 6000 BC. The times of the appearance of the various wheat species will probably have to be revised somewhat as future archaeological work takes place.

Although the earliest cultivation was apparently confined to the Near East, the wheats were soon to become widespread. Emmer was to become the principal wheat of ancient Egypt.\* From its early cultivation in the Balkans, wheat spread to other parts of Europe. One of the hexaploids, spelt, may have originated in central Europe, where it was prominent in prehistoric and early historical times. Other hexaploid wheats appeared in India, probably before the fourth millenium BC, and in China sometime before the beginning of the Christian era. Some people think mainly of rice in connection with India and China, but wheat early became important and continues to be so in the more temperate parts of these countries. The Spanish brought wheat to Mexico in 1529, and eventually the United States, Canada, and Argentina were to be among the world's greatest producers. (As token of the way technological and scientific development is drastically altering agricultural practice, it is interesting that the United States, where wheat is a relatively new crop, recently sent agricultural specialists to give advice on growing wheat in Turkey, where the crop has been grown for thousands of years.)

Wheat grows best in cool climates with little to moderate amounts of rain, and many areas of the earth's surface are suitable for its cultivation. Wheat is being harvested somewhere in the world every month of the year. Of the several species brought into domestication, only two are of major importance today: *Triticum aestivum*, used primarily for flour for bread and pastries, and *Triticum durum*, principally employed for making paste products such as macaroni, spaghetti, and noodles. Both species are cultivated in the United States, the latter principally in North Dakota. In the northern part of the United States and in Canada, wheat is planted in the spring; to the south of this area it is sown in the fall.

Although in some parts of the world the methods employed in growing, harvesting, and utilizing wheat are only little changed from those used in prehistoric times, in other places there have been great advances in wheat farming and in processing the grain—from the introduction of modern mechanical planting and harvesting to steamdriven rollers for milling. In the first part of this century it still took tremendous manpower to thresh and harvest wheat, even in the industrialized coun-

---

\*Occasionally an item is published in a newspaper to the effect that Mr. and Mrs. So-and-So on a vacation to Egypt visited the pyramids and brought home with them a few grains of "mummy" wheat, several thousand years old, and that the grains were planted and gave rise to healthy wheat plants. While it is true that grains of wheat dating back to pre-Christian times have been found in Egypt, there is no scientific verification of their ever germinating. Wheat seeds, like the seeds of most plants, have a rather short life, lasting only a few years.

tries, although some machinery was used. The combines used today consolidate what were formerly many separate operations of threshing and harvesting, and can be operated by a single person. The combine has thus led to drastic changes in farm life, including the virtual disappearance of the old "threshing party." Forty years ago straw stacks were a common sight on farms in the midwestern United States—now the straw is usually scattered on the fields in the combining process, or neatly baled. The straw, although of minor importance compared to the grain, has some uses. Though it is not a nutritious hay for livestock, wheat straw is unusually strong and has many uses on a farm; it can also be used by manufacturers as a filling for mattresses and in the making of paper and paper board.

Man's bread, too, has changed. To make a white flour, it is necessary to remove the germ and the bran from the grain. Technological advances in the milling process over the years have led to a whiter flour. Since the natural product is somewhat yellowish in color, a bleach is sometimes employed, and chemicals such as sodium propionate are sometimes added during the baking process to retard spoilage of the bread. Although white flours have superior keeping and baking qualities, they are much less nutritious than the whole wheat. Therefore the flour is often "enriched" by the addition of vitamins and minerals, which is required by law in some countries. These, however, fail to compensate for all the nutrients that have been removed from the grain. In the past a white bread was associated with the "higher" class or, at least, those with money. Recently there has been a trend toward whole-grain bread, at least among some of the better educated. It is a sad note on modern civilization that we must remove some of the nutrients and then supply additives to the product that goes on the table.

There have been changes in the wheat plant itself, as well as in methods of growing, harvesting, and milling it. Much of this evolution is the result of human selection and began when people first started growing the wild grasses. As the wild plant had a brittle fruiting stalk, the grains tended to fall individually as they matured, an advantage for seed dispersal in nature but undesirable for humans, who wanted to collect all the grains at one time. With domestication the fruiting stalk became less brittle, permitting the grains to remain on the plant. The cultivated plants developed seeds that would germinate rapidly and evenly, in contrast to the slower, more irregular germination of the seeds of the wild plant. The bracts surrounding the grain became more loosely attached, letting the grains fall free of the bracts during the harvest, which made it easier to prepare them for eating. There was

A

B

also some increase in the size of the grain. Numerous varieties of the different species came into existence through the agencies of mutation, hybridization, and both conscious and unconscious selection. Possibilities for hybridization increased as people moved from place to place or exchanged seeds with others.

As new varieties of wheat come into existence, some of the older ones tend to disappear, but many have existed little changed for hundreds of years. In this century plant breeders, through conscious selection and artificial hybridizations, have produced so many new varieties that there are now probably more than a thousand different kinds of bread wheat alone, some of them tailor-made for high productivity, special milling properties, adaptation to different climatic conditions, and resistance to disease.

Perhaps it is resistance to disease that has occupied as much of the plant breeder's attention as any other character. Practically all of the cultivated plants are subject to a number of diseases, and the wheat plant is particularly susceptible to stem rust, caused by a fungus that

C

*Figure 5–7* Traditional and modern methods of harvesting wheat. *A*. Threshing wheat with oxen in India. (Courtesy of Rockefeller Foundation.) *B*.Milling wheat in Pakistan. (Courtesy of FAO.) *C*. Combining wheat in the United States. (Courtesy of USDA.)

*Figure 5–8* Dr. Norman E. Borlaug (fourth from left) showing one of the new wheats developed in Mexico to a group of visiting scientists. (Courtesy of the Rockefeller Foundation.)

belongs to the same group as the common mushroom but is profoundly different in appearance. A severe infestation of stem rust can almost completely destroy a crop. Many races of wheat have been bred that are resistant to rusts, but the great difficulty is that there are also numerous races of rusts and new, more virulent ones continually come into existence through mutation and hybridization. Thus there will probably always be a need for the plant breeder to attempt to develop new resistant strains of wheat. Another accomplishment of plant breeders has been their contribution to the doubling of the wheat yield in the United States in the course of little more than a quarter of a century. Greater use of fertilizers and improved methods of preparing soil and eliminating weeds have also contributed to the increased yields.

Among the recent achievements of the wheat-plant breeder and other agricultural scientists is the remarkable work accomplished in Mexico that has contributed significantly to the Green Revolution. In 1943 members of the Rockefeller Foundation, at the invitation of the Mexican government, went to that country to see what could be done to increase food production. Although maize is the basic food plant of Mexico, wheat is very important also and Mexico was then importing half of the wheat it consumed. Much of the wheat being grown in Mexico at the time was little changed from that originally introduced by the Spanish in the early part of the sixteenth century. Working with Mexican agronomists, the scientists from the Rockefeller Foundation were able to double the yields in 20 years. A large part of the success resulted from the development through hybridization of rust-resistant varieties and semidwarf forms able to take heavy applications of fertilizer without falling over. The older, taller varieties tended to lodge, or fall over, when given sufficient fertilizer to increase the yields and thus could not be readily harvested. The parental type of the new semidwarf forms that have proved so successful originally came from the Orient. The first crop planted by Norman E. Borlaug, who headed the work for the Rockefeller Foundation and in 1970 received the Nobel Prize for his contributions to agriculture, was lost to rust. Fortunately, a few of the original seeds were still left in the seed envelopes, and these were grown the next year and used for the crosses that ultimately gave the kinds of plants that were wanted. Some of the wheat varieties developed for Mexico have proved to be successful in other parts of the world, and Pakistan is now producing enough wheat for its own needs, while India is approaching that goal. It is reported that in parts of India that used to produce seven or eight bushels an acre, yields of up to 60 or 70 bushels an acre are being secured by growing the new varieties under irrigation. In India the new high-yielding varieties originally attracted such attention that armed guards had to be posted at the experimental stations to prevent people from stealing seed before it was ready to be released to the public. Since wheat is a self-pollinated crop, once a hybrid has been stabilized and released to a farmer he can multiply his own seed stock for future planting.

Some years ago the Russians made great claims for a perennial wheat that could be grown from year to year without replanting. Through hybridization of a wheat with a perennial grass such a plant was actually made, but thus far it has been of little significance. Of much greater significance is the man-made hybrid between wheat and rye, first produced in Sweden. Although this plant was originally almost sterile, its fertility has been built up through selection. The hybrid, called triticale, or *Triticosecale* (from *Triticum*, wheat, and *Secale*, rye), gives grain that contains more and better protein than wheat, but the grain's low gluten content makes it less satisfactory than wheat for making bread. Triticale is now being grown as a crop in some regions, and research is continuing on this new cereal, particularly in Canada and Mexico.

*Figure 5–9*   Armed guard protecting plot of a new strain of wheat at an experimental station in India. It was necessary to post guards so that the farmers would not take the seeds before they were ready to be released to them. (Courtesy of Rockefeller Foundation.)

One of the next great "break-throughs" in wheat breeding may come with the production of a hybrid wheat that cashes in on the phenomenon of hybrid vigor—the increased yield of first-generation hybrids—as does maize, which is discussed later in this chapter. Hybridization, both natural and artificial, has been important in the development of the wheats, but it is far more difficult to accomplish than in maize, owing to the differences in the flowers of the two plants. Wheat has bisexual flowers and is normally self-pollinating, which makes the occurrence of hybridization an unusual event, whereas the sexes are separate on maize plants, and pollen is produced and dispersed much more freely than it is in wheat, so that the production of hybrids is a relatively simple matter. Cytoplasmic male-sterile lines, which have been very useful in making hybrid maize in recent years and are discussed later in the chapter, are now available in wheat, but there is still difficulty in securing hybrids because of wheat's natural breeding system.

Although it is always important to produce a plant that can yield more per acre, production of wheat was so great in the United States in the early 1960s that it included what has been referred to as an "embarrassing" surplus, more than could be utilized at home or sold for export. It has been easier to breed high-yielding wheats than it has been to solve the problems of their distribution.

## Rice

In Japan each year the Emperor himself, still patron of all agriculture although no longer regarded as the descendant of the sun, joins in the ritual harvest of the rice on the small imperial paddy field in the palace grounds. Rice is still regarded as a sacred plant by many people in much of Asia. Although of more limited distribution than wheat, rice feeds more people, since it constitutes the basic food of more than half of humankind.

Far less is known about the origin of rice than about the origins of the other important cereals, but there is little doubt that its cultivation arose in southeastern Asia, where it continues to be of paramount importance. Archaeological evidence from Thailand and China suggests that rice was domesticated around 4000 BC, but it could be that this actually occurred even earlier, for the archaeological record of plants from this part of the world is much poorer than it is for the Near East and the Americas.

Rice reached Japan from China during the second century BC. At this time it was already known in Europe, for it had been carried to Greece by Arab traders and again during Alexander the Great's invasion of the East. The scientific name *Oryza*, applied to the plant by Linnaeus, comes from an ancient Greek word for rice that, in turn, is derived from either an Arabic word or a Chinese word—opinion is divided among scholars. The Chinese word means "good grain of life"; not surprisingly, the word for rice is the same as that for life, food, or agriculture in many parts of the Far East. Rice is mentioned in very ancient Chinese writings, as it is in early Hindu scriptures. Several different varieties of rice are described in the ancient Dravidian literature of India. Linguistic evidence, as well as botanical, suggests an origin for the plant somewhere in southeastern Asia.

There are twenty species of *Oryza* and of these, one species, *Oryza sativa*, furnishes virtually all of the rice of the world today. A second domesticated species, *Oryza glaberrima*, is still cultivated in West Africa, presumably in the same area where it originated. There is yet no agreement as to the ancestral species; *Oryza rufipogon*, a perennial, and

*Figure 5–10* Rice. (Courtesy of FAO.)

*Oryza nivara*, an annual, both widespread in southern Asia, have been suggested. These and similar species of wild rice* presumably were collected by primitive people, just as wheat was, and eventually became intentionally grown. With cultivation mutant types were selected, and

---

*There is another plant known as wild rice that is also used for food; although a grass, it is not very closely related to true rice, *Oryza*. This wild rice, *Zizania aquatica*, is an annual, native to eastern North America, and was an important noncultivated food plant of the Indians of the Great Lakes region, particularly in what is now Minnesota, Wisconsin, and Manitoba. It is still collected by Indians for their own use and as a cash crop. At one point outsiders introduced mechanical means of harvesting the crop that could have proved disastrous if their use had gone unchecked. The more primitive methods always left plenty of seeds to reestablish the plants for the next season, but with the more efficient mechanical method, most of the seeds were collected and the species was threatened with extinction. Fortunately, some laws governing the harvest were passed in time, and the plant still survives. Attempts are now being made to establish it as a cultivated plant.

in time an annual was produced, with larger grains and nonshattering fruit stalks, and sometimes lacking the awns of the wild species. Hybridization of the cultivated rice with various wild species also appears to have contributed to the development and the great variability of this plant. Wild rice is still collected by some people, and is the preferred plant in some ancient religious ceremonies in southeastern Asia. Although some tetraploid races are known, most varieties of rice are diploid, having 24 chromosomes.

Rice was introduced into the Carolinas in 1647, but today California, Arkansas, Louisiana, and Texas are the rice-growing areas of the United States; more than half of the rice produced goes for export. As the consumption of rice in the United States is only six pounds per person per year, not a great deal need be produced to meet the domestic demand. Some rice is grown in Africa, South America, and Europe, and it is an important food in many places. In many parts of Latin America, rice and beans are served with every meal, and sometimes they constitute the whole meal. But it is in its original homeland that rice is dominant, where more than 90 percent of the world's crop is produced, and where the average person consumes as much rice in a week as the average American eats in a whole year.

Throughout much of southeastern Asia, rice is grown as it has been for many centuries, requiring tremendous human effort. It has been estimated that in some regions one thousand man-hours are needed to grow and harvest a single acre of rice. A great many people still cultivate very small patches—from one to five acres—of rice.

As methods vary somewhat from region to region, a generalized description is impossible, but the following steps are very common. The paddy fields are prepared for planting with a wooden single-furrow plow, drawn by a water buffalo or ox. Manure, if available, is scattered on the field. The plowed land is then smoothed with a log. After the dikes have been repaired, river water drawn by primitive water wheels is used to flood the fields in areas where rain is not sufficient for this purpose.

The rice is then planted, either by broadcasting dry or previously germinated seed, or by transplanting seedlings or young plants that have been grown in a nursery bed. The customary way of planting most cereals is directly by seed, and knowledge of the origin of transplanting seedlings by hand would be of interest. Carl Sauer has postulated that the latter is the older method, first used by people who had practiced vegetative cultivation of noncereal crops, transplanting being similar to starting plants from cuttings or by other vegetative means. Broadcasting dry seeds might have been derived from contact

*Figure 5–11* Terraced paddy fields in Indonesia. Mechanization would be difficult in this kind of terrain. (Courtesy of FAO.)

with wheat farmers at a later date. It is not definitely known which is the older method. Transplanting, backbreaking work that requires much stooping, is usually done by women and children. Some pruning of the tops and the roots of plants normally accompanies transplantation, and some people believe that this pruning stimulates growth of the young plant and leads to higher yields than when seeds are broadcast. Weeds present less of a problem when rice is transplanted than when seed is planted directly, and having less competition from weeds could also help account for greater yields being obtained through the transplanting method. After the plants are established, any necessary weeding is done by hand, another activity that requires much stooping.

A

B

*Figure 5–12*  *A*. Farmer hoeing a paddy field in Indonesia. Although water buffalo (Figure 4–9) are widely used, much hand labor still goes into the preparation and care of the fields. *B*. Transplanting rice seedlings in Japan. (Courtesy of FAO.)

Harvesting is done with sickles or knives. With the latter the seed heads are gently cut individually, for the idea still exists in some regions that if the cutting is harsh, the rice plant will be offended and the yield will be decreased the following season. Threshing is done by beating the heads against the ground or against logs, or by having animals or barefoot humans tread upon the seed heads. Sometimes women who do the treading are barebreasted, which is thought to be related to an ancient belief that the less they wear, the thinner the rice husks will be. Winnowing to remove the chaff from the grain is still often accomplished by tossing the rice from bamboo or rattan trays and allowing the wind to blow away the lighter chaff while the grain settles nearby. All of these methods, of course, contrast strikingly with the highly mechanized procedures practiced in the United States and some other countries, where airplanes are sometimes employed for seeding, allowing the grain to be produced economically in spite of high labor costs.

Following winnowing, under primitive conditions, a mortar and pestle are used for hulling and the brown rice that results may be promptly cooked for local consumption. In industrial preparation, pearling or whitening removes the bran, or outer layers of the grain, and sometimes polishing follows. The final product is pleasing in appearance and taste but less nutritious than brown rice. Unfortunately, just as with bread, most people prefer white rice to brown. The loss of nutrients, particularly vitamin $B_1$, eliminated in the process of milling and cooking, has been responsible for deficiency diseases such as beriberi among people whose diet consists almost entirely of white rice. Highly milled rice contains only 0.04 milligrams of vitamin $B_1$ per 100 grams, compared to 0.4 milligrams in unmilled rice; the latter amount is sufficient to prevent beriberi in someone who eats rice daily. White rice, of course, can be fortified with additives to increase its nutritional value.

Rice, although not a true aquatic plant, is unusual among the cereals in that its roots can thrive under water. Thus it is an ideal plant for much of the humid tropics, although at times it can get too much water, for proper drainage is essential to its good growth. The presence of a weed, the water fern, *Azolla*, in rice paddies has long been known to stimulate the growth of rice. It was found that the water fern is inhabited by the blue-green alga, *Anabaena*, which supplies nitrogen to the rice through its ability to fix atmospheric nitrogen.* The Chinese are now deliberately planting the water fern in rice fields, thus eliminating the need for expensive nitrogenous fertilizer. Rice also can be grown much

---

*See page 128.

A

B

*Figure 5–13* *A.* Winnowing rice in Burma. (Courtesy of FAO.) *B.* Hulling and pounding maize in Cambodia. Many of the traditional implements used for rice have been adopted for maize in this part of the world. Banana plants in background. (Courtesy of FAO.)

as the other cereals. Dry upland rice, or hill paddy, is grown in some areas that have the proper temperature and sufficient rainfall. Yields, however, are generally lower than for lowland rice.

The thousands of "varieties" of rice are generally divided into two major groups—the *japonica* types, which have short grains and are sticky when cooked, and the *indica* types, which have long grains and are drier when cooked. The *japonica* types, grown in both Japan and Taiwan, in general are higher yielding than are the *indica* types, which are grown throughout the greater part of southeastern Asia. World hunger could be at least partially reduced through the wider distribution of the higher yielding varieties. One of the obstacles to achieving this goal, however, lies in the difficulty of persuading people to accept new foods. People the world over usually prefer their local staples, and if they are used to eating a sticky rice, for example, they are often reluctant to change to a dry type, and vice versa.

The rice plant, directly or indirectly serves humankind in many ways other than for food. Beers and wines may be made from the grain, the most famous of which is *sake*, the "national beverage" of Japan. Rice is also used in the manufacture of beer in the United States and other countries. Rice is used for the production of starch, and rice powder is used as a cosmetic in parts of the Far East. The hulls, or husks, of the grain are used as fuel, in making building materials, for the manufacture of the chemical furfural, which in turn is used to make plastics, and in other ways. The straw, of course, is not overlooked and is used in the manufacture of baskets, mats, and strawboard. Like wheat straw, rice straw is not very nutritious, but it is sometimes used for livestock feed. Paper can be made from rice straw, but what is commonly known as rice paper is made from another plant—*Tetrapanax papyriferus*, or rice-paper plant—which is native to the Orient but is not a grass.

Perhaps the most important by-product of rice farming doesn't come from the plant itself, for paddy fields are frequently used for raising fish. A rice diet is extremely deficient in protein, and fish, of course, is an excellent protein source. In many rice-growing areas ponds are kept for fish hatcheries, and small fish, usually carp, are introduced into the paddy fields. The fish, rather than decreasing rice production, actually appear to promote its fertility. Without the fish in the wet rice fields, other problems may arise—as was discovered in the south coastal area of the United States some years ago when huge swarms of mosquitoes found the rice fields ideal breeding grounds. In parts of Asia the recent use of modern pesticides has had a deleterious effect on the fish populations.

Of the many diseases of rice, one has proven to be of particular scientific interest. The *bakanae* or "foolish seedling" disease, which produces unusually tall, thin plants, was found by Japanese botanists to be caused by a fungus, *Gibberella fujikuroi*. They found that a growth substance, now known as gibberellin, could be isolated from the fungus, and this substance has been the subject of considerable scientific work by American and English botanists as well as the Japanese since World War II. Gibberellins are used to produce growth in some dwarf plants and to induce flowering in others.

Although some efforts to improve the rice plant have been carried on for many years, and high-yielding strains have been grown in Japan and Formosa, much of Asia still grows its old unproductive types under very primitive conditions. Recognizing the need for improvement in a plant that feeds a great part of the world's population, the Ford Foundation, in cooperation with the Rockefeller Foundation, established the International Rice Research Institute in the Philippines. With scientists representing many different disciplines assembled from the United States and six Asian nations, the IRRI began its work in 1962. It was soon found that, although rice was a much studied plant, there was still much room for basic research. Effort was devoted to learning more about the plant, and this search for basic knowledge still continues.

It was known that one of the great drawbacks of rice was its tendency to lodge, or fall over, as the plants reached maturity. Fertilization, which would improve yields of such plants, would only contribute to lodging since it would produce taller plants with heavier heads. The rice scientists realized that an ideal rice plant would be a short one with a strong stem, that could take additional amounts of fertilizer. Over 10,000 different samples of rice seed from many different areas were assembled, and through hybridization the IRRI scientists attempted to produce a plant having the desirable characters. One of the crosses, involving a short rice from Taiwan called Deegeowoogen and one from Indonesia called Peta, gave extremely high yields, not only in the Far East but in South America and Africa as well. The new plant, designated IR8, reaches maturity in 130 days and is insensitive to day length, making it adaptable to many regions and making it possible to grow more than one crop a year in some places. Other high-yielding varieties have since been developed. The IRRI did not neglect other aspects of growing rice—fertilization, irrigation, disease control—and even produced an inexpensive threshing machine that could be widely used.

Thus, in the space of a few years, through a highly concentrated effort, rice yields have increased dramatically and are already contributing to the Green Revolution. What is still needed is a rice that has a higher protein content, for rice contains even less protein than wheat and maize, and the newly produced varieties may have protein contents even lower than that of some of the older, low-yielding varieties.

## Maize, or Indian Corn

From a plant that was once used mostly to feed people, maize has become one of the world's chief feeds for animals. Maize, however, still retains its role as a basic human food plant in parts of the Americas. It is generally held that maize was not known in the Old World until after some of Columbus' men found it growing in Cuba. Maize was already several thousands of years old at the time, and it had fed the laborers who built magnificent temples in Mexico and Peru in prehistoric times; today, directly or indirectly, it supplies much of the energy for technological developments in the United States.

At the time of the Discovery, maize was the most widely grown plant in the Americas, extending from southern Canada to southern South America, growing at sea level in some places and at elevations higher than 11,000 feet in others. Woodlands were cleared, swamps drained, deserts irrigated, and terraces built on mountain sides so that the plant could be grown, but little maize grew in the area that was to become the great corn belt of the United States, for not until the mould board plow was invented would it be possible to turn the heavy prairie sod. For many years after America was discovered by Europeans, much of the future corn belt was to continue to be dominated by wild grasses and buffalo.

Much of American Indian life centered on maize, the "gift of the gods," just as it still does today in parts of Mexico and other Latin American countries. In religion and art, as well as in everyday life, many human activities were concerned with the maize plant. For food, it was popped—probably one of the oldest ways of preparing the hard grain—parched, boiled, or ground. By washing the grains in wood ashes and quicklime, the Indians made maize into hominy. Ground, it was used for making unleavened "bread", or tortillas. It was also eaten green; from quids, or chewed wads, recovered in archaeological deposits, we know that this is one of the most ancient methods of eating it. Sometimes even the pollen was added to soups or stews, and corn smut, a fungus disease that affects corn, was also eaten. As Paul Weatherwax has written, "Perhaps the most cheering and heart-warming use

*Figure 5–14* Indian methods of preparing bread and chicha. (From Jerónimo Benzoni, 1565.)

the Indians made of maize was the production of alcoholic beverages." It was probably early learned that a nutritious beverage could be made by chewing or germinating the grain to start a process of fermentation. The beer, or *chicha*, that results is still widely made and used in South America, although in many areas, unfortunately, it has been replaced by the much more potent and less nutritious sugar-cane alcoholic beverage, *aguardiente*. The Indians also found many uses for parts of the plant other than the grain, as they still do.

In Europe maize was first grown as a curiosity, like many other American plants of the time. To distinguish it from the other cereals, it was at first called Turkey corn or Turkey wheat, because some people thought that it came from that country.* An American Indian name, *maize*, or *mays*, was used to some extent. Linnaeus, the great Swedish botanist of the eighteenth century who named many of our plants, adopted it for the specific designation of the plant and used *zea*, an ancient Greek word for cereal, as the genus name. Thus we still have *Zea mays* as the scientific name of maize.

The new plant was not exactly a rousing success in all parts of Europe. John Gerard, the famous English herbalist of the late sixteenth and early seventeenth century, had this to say:

> Turky wheat doth nourish far lesse than either wheat, rie, barly, or otes. The bread which is made thereof is meanely white, without bran: it is hard and dry as Bisket is, and hath in it no clamminesse at all; for which

*Some people have maintained that maize reached Asia before Columbus discovered America, and that it may have entered Europe by way of Turkey.

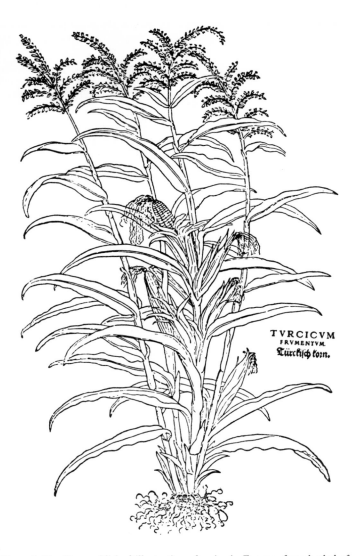

*Figure 5–15*  First published illustration of maize in Europe, from herbal of Leonhard Fuchs, 1542. Fuchs believed that the plant came from Asia and called it Turkish corn.

cause it is of hard digestion, and yeeldeth to the body little or no nourishment. Wee have as yet not certaine proofe or experience concerning
the vertues of this kinde of corne; although the barbarous Indians, which
know no better, are constrained to make a vertue of necessitie, and thinke
it a good food: whereas we may easily judge, that it nourisheth but little,
and is of hard and evill digestion, a more convenient food for swine than
for man.

More than two centuries later, the English imported corn to Ireland
from America as food for the Irish people during the great famine. The
Irish did not take readily to the new food. They did not know how to
prepare it, they had no good implements for grinding it, and when
they did, they didn't like the taste. Their inability to accept and use
a new World plant is rather ironic, for it was the failure of the potato
crop that led to the famine, and the potato had been introduced to
Europe from the Americas even later than maize.

Indeed, the maize plant was a strange one to the Europeans—an
amazing plant, if you will excuse an old pun—quite unlike the other
cereals known to them. Not only was it larger, but instead of bearing
its grains in a head at the top of the plant, it bore them in ears on the
sides of the stalk, with the silks, or styles, protruding. At the top it
produced tassels, which, except in exceptional circumstances, produced
only male flowers. The grains, instead of being covered individually
by chaff as in other cereals, were naked,* and the ear as a whole was
covered by husks. Although nearly all domesticated plants are poorly
equipped to survive in the wild, maize is even more helpless than most,
because the grains remain attached to the cob. Maize had to be handled
differently for planting than the cereals familiar to the Europeans.
Instead of being broadcast over the field, maize grains, which are much
larger than those of other cereals, were planted individually. This
method of planting may relate to a basic difference in very early agriculture between the Old and the New Worlds. In the Old World
people had animals to plow the fields in preparation for the broadcasting
of seed, whereas in the New World the only animal available was man
himself, and what crude preparation the field received was done with
a digging stick or hoe. The maize farmer would have focused more

---

*There is a rather rare form of maize, known as pod corn, in which the individual
grains are covered.

104

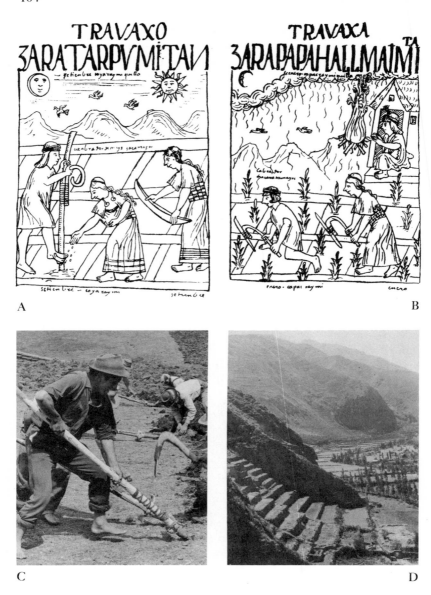

*Figure 5–16* Growing maize in Peru. *A*. Planting. Footplow is used to break soil.
*B*. Cultivating. (From Poma de Ayala, c. 1600 AD.) *C*. Preparing a field for planting
today. Note similarity of plow to that shown in *A*. (Courtesy of FAO.) *D*. Terraces.
Many of the terraces constructed by the Incas are still in use at present. (Courtesy of
Paul Weatherwax.)

attention on the individual plant, for which he had carefully sown a single seed, than did the wheat farmer who had broadcast seed; this may have been significant in the evolution of maize, for attention paid to variant individuals may help explain its great diversity.

Maize is certainly a most variable species, probably more so than any other plant. Many people are well aware of the great variation in the color of the grains, since multicolored ears are often used as decorations. The kernels also vary considerably in size and shape, as do the ears, which may range from a little over one inch to a foot and a half long. Some varieties are known that reach maturity in a little over two months, whereas others require more than a year. For convenience, five main types of maize are recognized: (1) popcorn, probably the most primitive type, with extremely hard grains that allow pressure to be built up within them upon heating; "popping" results when the sudden expansion of the soft starch turns the grain inside out (other varieties of maize and other cereals can also be popped and are commonly prepared in this way as breakfast foods, but special methods are necessary to allow the pressure to build up); (2) flint corns, which have kernels of hard starch; (3) flour corns, which have soft starch, of particular value to the Indians because it is easily ground, but disadvantageous in being quite subject to insect damage; (4) dent corns, so called because there is a dent in the top of the kernel in which a soft starch overlies an area of hard starch; modern dent corns are responsible for the high productivity of the corn belt, and were originated in the nineteenth century by crossing a southern dent corn with a northern flint variety; and (5) sweet corn, which has sugary instead of starchy kernels, and is today a favorite fresh vegetable. There is also another type of corn, called waxy corn, that is distinguished by a starch that is chemically different from that of other corns. It receives its name from the waxlike appearance of the grain when it is cut. Waxy corn was discovered in China at the beginning of this century and has come to have some special uses in industry and for food because of its very different kind of starch. In spite of this great variability, all maize is regarded by botanists as belonging to a single species. All the varieties are diploid, having ten pairs of chromosomes.

Where this species came from has long been a question of great interest to botanists, and at times proponents of different views have had rather heated arguments. Although much remains to be learned, there now appears to be some general agreement about where maize must have originated and the approximate time when this occurred, as well as about what happened to the plant under human influence. There

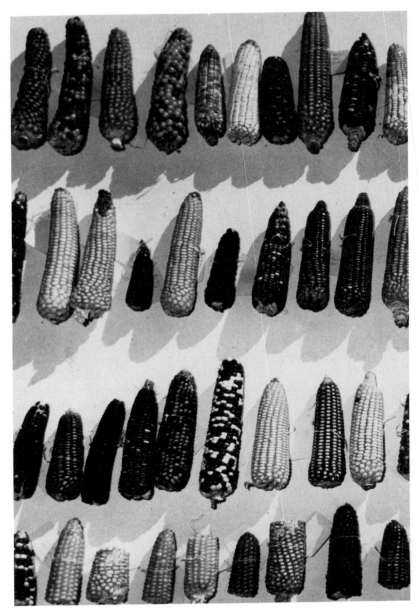

*Figure 5–17A* A collection of maize from Guatemala showing some of the great variation found in this plant. (Courtesy of USDA.)

*Figure 5–17B* Principal varieties of maize. (Left to right: popcorn, sweet corn, flour corn, flint corn, dent corn, pod corn. (Courtesy of USDA.)

also appears to be growing agreement about what plant gave rise to maize.

It has been known since the last century that teosinte, a coarse annual* wild grass of Mexico, Guatemala, and Honduras, now becoming rather rare, was the closest relative of maize. The two plants cross naturally and produce fertile hybrids. Teosinte was originally considered to belong to a distinct genus and was classified as *Euchlaena mexicana*. The later recognition of its very close relationship with maize prompted its transfer to the genus *Zea*, and quite recently the proposal has been made that it belongs to the same species as maize. The idea that teosinte might be the ancestor of maize is not a new one, but it was largely ignored for a number of years in favor of a much more spectacular hypothesis of the origin of maize.

---

*Recently a new perennial teosinte has been discovered in southern Jalisco, Mexico (H. H. Iltis, *et al.*, *Science* 203: 186–188, 1979.) that may have important implications bearing on the origin of maize and may prove useful in breeding.

The view that teosinte was not an ancestor of maize but a hybrid that had maize as one of its parents was developed by Paul Mangelsdorf and R. G. Reeves. Their hypothesis, advanced in 1939, proposed that maize had originated in South America from a wild form of pod corn. It was introduced by man into Central America and Mexico, where it encountered the wild gamagrass *Tripsacum*. Hybridization took place between maize and *Tripsacum*, and as a result of this hybridization teosinte was created. Hybridization later took place between maize and teosinte, producing superior varieties of maize. In support of their hypothesis they pointed out that pod corn, which had a natural means of dispersal for the grains, could be construed as the wild type; that the Andes could be regarded as the place of origin because there the greatest variability in maize is found;* and that teosinte is in many respects intermediate between maize and *Tripsacum*, as might be expected of a hybrid.

Since 1939 new evidence, particularly archaeological, bearing on the origin of maize has come to light. Pollen discovered under Mexico City, dated as being 80,000 years old, was identified as that of maize. One of the most interesting discoveries came from Tehuacan, where cobs of maize only little more than half an inch long (Figure 1–1) were found in deposits dated between 5000 and 3400 BC. The new evidence led Mangelsdorf in 1974 to revise his hypothesis concerning the origin of maize. While still contending that the ancestor of corn was a wild pod corn now extinct, he now considers corn to have had several independent domestications both in Mexico and in South America. He no longer considers teosinte to be of hybrid origin but rather a mutant derivative of maize. The earliest cobs from Tehuacan he believes to belong to a wild maize. A number of other investigators, however, have recently concluded that teosinte is indeed the progenitor of corn. If this is so, there is no need to postulate that wild maize ever became extinct, for teosinte and wild maize are the same plant. The earliest cobs recovered from Tehuacan, according to most of the proponents of this hypothesis, represent an early domesticated form of maize. Corn, therefore, originated in Mexico and was carried as a domesticated plant to South America.

One of the stumbling blocks in the acceptance of teosinte as the ancestor of maize was that it was difficult to understand how people

---

*The idea that the center of diversity of a cultivated plant usually indicates its place of origin was formulated by N. I. Vavilov, a Russian scientist who made many contributions to our understanding of domesticated plants. Today it is realized, however, that there are often other explanations for centers of diversity.

*Figure 5–18*  *A.* Teosinte. (Reprinted with permission of The Macmillion Company from Paul Weatherwax, *Indian Corn in Old America*. Copyright © 1954 by The Macmillan Company.) *B.* Teosinte ear on left, about three inches long. Husks removed to show single row of grains on right. The grains are separate at maturity and fall individually.

could have used its extremely hard grains for food. Shortly after the publication of the original Mangelsdorf-Reeves paper, George Beadle, who did not accept the hybrid origin of teosinte, showed that grains of teosinte could be popped like those of popcorn and pointed out that primitive people could have used it in such a fashion. Early written accounts have since been found indicating that teosinte grains were parched for eating. That man ever took such a seemingly unpromising food plant and made it into one of the world's greatest cereals may strain the belief of some, but this hypothesis has gained a number of adherents in the last few years.

Although presumably maize was a most mutable plant, it must have required considerable conscious selection to have produced the great number of races that existed when it was discovered by the Europeans. The development of a wild grass into the "happy monster" that once fed most of the people of the Americas was a most significant achievement of primitive plant breeders. The development of hybrid corn in this century ranks as one of the most outstanding developments of the modern plant breeder.

The story of hybrid corn has been told many times and in many places but it bears retelling. First, some general remarks about hybridization are in order, to set the stage. Hybridization has already been mentioned several times in this book—both natural hybridization (between and within species) and man-made, or artificial, hybridization for plant and animal improvement. In either natural or artificial hybridization, genes may pass from one species or variety into another as a result of the backcrossing of the first generation $(F_1)$ hybrid to one of its parent types; the new types that result may be exploited by man. Such gene transfer may occur from many hybrids between species, but not from all of them by any means, for some interspecific hybrids are sterile or nearly so, like the mule. On the other hand, hybrids within a species, for example, between two different varieties, are generally fertile; this is true of hybrids between different varieties of maize. One other important characteristic of hybrids has already been mentioned: First-generation hybrids frequently show a greater vigor than either of their parents. This *hybrid vigor*, also called *heterosis*, is seen in the mule, and was to prove to be one of the greatest significance in corn.

Two of our greatest biologists, Charles Darwin and Gregor Mendel, figure at least indirectly in the production of hybrid maize. Darwin in some of his researches found that continual inbreeding of plants reduced vigor, whereas crossing different varieties increased vigor. Darwin even used maize in some of his experiments, although nothing more was to come of it at the time. Mendel supplied us with the laws of genetics that, after their rediscovery in 1900, made it possible to use deliberate planning in developing better plants and animals.

The history of hybrid corn begins with a man much influenced by Darwin, William James Beal, who in 1877 made the first controlled crosses in maize in an attempt to increase the yield. In his work at Michigan Agricultural College (now Michigan State University) he proved that yields could be increased by crossing different varieties. Shortly after the turn of the century two researchers began to study the effects of inbreeding: George Harrison Shull at Cold Spring Har-

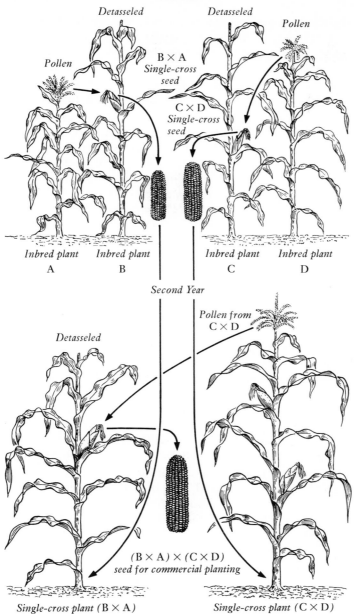

*Figure 5–19* Double-cross method of producing hybrid-corn seed. The inbreds shown at the top are crossed to produce seed that gives the single-cross hybrids shown below. The single-cross plants are then crossed to produce double-crossed seed to be sold to the farmer. (From "Hybrid Corn" by Paul C. Mangelsdorf. Copyright © 1951 by Scientific American, Inc. All rights reserved.)

bor, New York, who was following up some of Mendel's discoveries, and Edmund Murray East at the Connecticut Experiment Station. Their self-pollinated maize plants became weaker after each generation, but they found that if two inbred varieties were crossed, great vigor could be restored in this single step. The final touches for the ultimate commercial production of hybrid corn were provided by D. F. Jones, a student of East at Harvard, who went to the Connecticut Experiment Station in 1914. The inbreds were very weak plants* and produced rather small ears with few seeds. Thus, if inbred A were pollinated by inbred B, the seeds produced on A would be used for hybrids, but its small number of seeds made it of little practical use. Jones devised a double cross using four inbreds: A was crossed with B, and C with D, and the resulting hybrids AB and CD were then grown and a cross made between them. The resulting plant, being a hybrid, produced a large number of seeds, and these double-crossed seeds still produced plants showing extreme vigor and uniformity. By utilizing the double cross, it was now possible to convert a few bushels of single-crossed seed into 1000 bushels of double-crossed seed that could then be released to the farmer, making it economically feasible to grow hybrid corn. Thus, through the work of several scientists in addition to those mentioned here, and of practical farmers as well, hybrid corn became a reality. The double-cross method for production of hybrid-corn seed is still employed, but gradually, as better inbreds have been developed, single crosses have come more and more into use for the production of hybrid seed for direct sale to the farmer. In 1970 seventy-five percent of the hybrid corn grown in the United States was derived from single crosses.

By careful selection of the inbreds, a breeder can produce high-yielding maize hybrids for many different climatic zones. Special characters, such as resistance to disease and tolerance to drought, can be incorporated, as well as special morphological features. Plants have been developed that produce two or three ears to the plant instead of one, uniformly placed on the stalk to make harvesting by mechanical pickers practical. Plants with stiff stalks have been produced to withstand mechanical picking. Hybrid-corn seed must be purchased anew each year, for if a farmer saved seeds from one year's crop for planting the next, he would lose much of the vigor and uniformity found in the

---

*In fact, the inbreds were such sick-looking plants that in the early days of hybrid corn development in at least one agricultural experiment station they were grown in out-of-the-way places where farmers would be unlikely to see them. The breeders felt that if the farmers saw the inbreds they would think the breeders were working in the wrong direction.

original hybrids. Thus, the production of hybrid-corn seed became big business in the United States.

The changeover to use of hybrid corn was slow initially. Only one percent of the corn produced in the United States in 1935 was hybrid, but today virtually all the corn grown in this country is hybrid. Hybrid corn soon made possible the production on three acres what used to be produced on four. Equally important is the fact that hybrid corn has made possible a drastic reduction in the number of man-hours required to produce a bushel of corn. The increased yields with reduced manpower were particularly important during World War II when, with a serious depletion of the labor force, the amount of corn produced decreased by only 10 percent. Since the war, yields have continued to increase dramatically, more than doubling in the space of 20 years. It should, of course, be obvious that other scientific advances have contributed to the great increase in corn production.

Hybrid maize has become important in other parts of the world and is gradually replacing the old types of maize grown in Latin America, with great increases in yield. Yugoslavia became a maize producer by importing hybrid-corn seed from Iowa. Seldom can a plant well adapted to one area be an immediate success in another, but Yugoslavia, being at the same latitude as Iowa and having a climate not too dissimilar, was able to take immediate advantage of the introduced seeds.

In the production of seed for hybrid corn the seed companies grow a row of one inbred, A, to be the male parent, next to another, B, that is to serve as the female, or seed, parent. In order to insure that self-pollination of B does not occur, it is necessary to remove its tassels before pollen is shed. In the early years of seed production, this operation of detasselling was done by hand, college students often being employed for the work. One of the recent advances in hybrid-seed production has been the elimination of detasselling through the discovery of plants that produce no pollen. The factor for pollen sterility, referred to as cytoplasmic male sterility, resides in the cytoplasm of the cell rather than in the nucleus and is inherited quite differently from ordinary Mendelian genes. Since plants derived from a male-sterile parent produce no pollen, it is necessary for a breeder to introduce a gene into the hybrids to make the next generation pollen-fertile. Virtually all the hybrid seed now sold in the United States is produced by utilization of plants carrying the male sterility factor along with genes for restoring fertility when the seed is grown by the farmer.*

---

*Hybrids containing the male-sterile cytoplasmic factor were seriously affected by blight in 1970; see footnote page 218.

It will perhaps come as no surprise to learn that nowhere in the world is more maize produced than in the United States. Argentina is second in production and China is probably third. Maize is also of considerable importance in many other parts of the Old World, for in spite of the reluctance to accept it in some places, next to tobacco, it was the New World plant most widely adopted following the European discovery of America. Although its cultivation in the United States is concentrated in a relatively few states extending from western Ohio to eastern Kansas and Nebraska, maize is, by yield, the single most important crop plant in the United States. It ranks behind several other crops in export value, so obviously most of it is used at home. In fact, some 80 percent of the crop never leaves the farm but is used directly for livestock food. The small amount that does go to market is extremely important and yields more products than any other cereal. Practically all parts of the corn plant are used in some way, but only the grain has significant use. A few years ago a survey of a supermarket revealed that the grain was used in one way or another in the preparation of 197 different food products sold there, and if the drug counter had been included in the survey many other products would have been added, for corn starch is used as a filler for aspirin and other tablets, and corn syrup is used as a base for cough medicines. Some 200 million bushels go to the corn refineries, or "wetmillers," every year; here the oil-bearing germ, or embryo, is removed, then the outer covering, the gluten, and finally the starch, which constitutes more than half of the kernel. The starch is used directly, as cornstarch, or is converted into syrups or sugar. Cornstarch is sold for use in food, drugs, and cosmetics and for other industrial uses. The syrups and sugars also find a great number of uses: in foods, in the preparation of medicine, in chewing gum and soft drinks, and in making cold-rubber tires. The solubles from the steep water left after removal of other substances find many uses, as do the glutens—in animal feeds and in the manufacture of plastics, for example. The refined oil from the germ is used in cooking, in salad dressings, and in the making of margarine. Perhaps other plants, such as soybeans and coconuts, have more uses than maize, but certainly maize would run them a close race.

Research is constantly underway to find new uses for maize and to improve the plant, for maize has a badly balanced protein and, like rice, a lower protein content than wheat. It is also a poor source of certain vitamins. The deficiency disease pellagra, caused by a shortage of the vitamin niacin, is often found among people whose diet is inadequate. Large amounts of the amino acid tryptophan have a niacinlike

*Figure 5–20* Grinding maize, Mexico. (Reprinted with permission of The Macmillan Company from Paul Weatherwax, *Indian Corn in Old America.* Copyright © 1954 by The Macmillan Company.)

affect in the body and may partially substitute for niacin. Since maize is deficient in both the vitamin and the amino acid, pellagra is common among some peoples who depend on it as their staple. How then did the American Indian fare so well where maize was the principal food? Throughout much of the Americas the Indians prepared their maize using lime—from wood ashes, shells or other sources. For example, tortillas are prepared by cooking the dried kernels in a weak solution of lime water for a half hour or more, after which the corn is ground to yield a *masa*, or dough. It has recently been shown that the use of heat with lime enhances the balance of the amino acids in maize and frees the small amount of niacin, which is otherwise unavailable. It is unlikely that the Indians were aware that this method of preparing maize increased its nutritive value; the procedure was probably adopted because they found that the hard kernels were softened by the lime water and could be ground more easily. How they happened on this happy discovery remains unknown. In 1964, scientists at Purdue University discovered that a mutant maize called opaque-2, which had been known for more than a quarter of a century, had a significantly

*Figure 5–21*   Grain sorghum.

higher lysine and tryptophan content than other types. Increases in these two amino acids greatly improves the nutritive value of maize, and in a protein-hungry world this discovery could be more significant than any new industrial use for maize. Field tests in Colombia have already indicated that the new maize may have a significant impact on protein deficiency in that country.

As a botanist, I cannot close this discussion without mention of another important, although sometimes overlooked, use of maize—in teaching and research. In the development of modern genetics, maize has been to the botanist what the fruit fly *Drosophila* has been to the zoologist. It is a particularly valuable plant because its chromosomes are exceptionally large, which has allowed detailed studies that have contributed greatly to our understanding of inheritance.

## Sorghum

Grain sorghum (*Sorghum bicolor*), a cereal somewhat resembling maize in vegetative features and bearing its grain in a terminal cluster, feeds millions of people in Africa and Asia. It is more drought tolerant than

*Figure 5–22*   Broom corn.

most cereals, hence it is of great importance in semiarid regions that will not support the growth of the major cereal plants. It is generally regarded as having been domesticated in Africa, where wild forms of the species are known; the savanna zone of eastern Africa, north of the equator, has been suggested as the place of origin. Some have held, however, that it was first domesticated in India. Archaeological sorghum grains from India date to 1800 BC, far earlier than any archaeological material thus far reported from Africa. Only recently has grain sorghum become an important crop in the United States, being grown mainly in the Southwest and used mostly for animal feed. Most grain sorghums now grown in the United States are hybrids developed through the use of cytoplasmic male-sterile lines.

In addition to the development of plants with large amounts of grain, man has also selected *Sorghum bicolor* for other uses, in which the emphasis is on parts other than the grains. The sweet sorghums, or sorgos, which have a high concentration of sugar in the stem, are used for making syrups or for forage. The grass sorghums, such as Tunis grass, have been selected for high yields of foliage, which is used for feeding livestock. Broomcorn is a sorghum grown for the stalks that are used to make brooms and brushes.

# 6

# Sugar

*Things sweet to taste prove in digestion sour.*
William Shakespeare, *King Richard II*

Perhaps even more than meat, sugar is a luxury food. We can live without it, but it has always been in great demand because of the enjoyment it adds to eating. Two plants, sugar cane and sugar beet, furnish most of our sugar, although many other plants provide small amounts. Two of these, maize and sorghum, were treated in the last chapter. Several palms provide sugar in southeastern Asia. Maple sugar from the sugar maple (*Acer saccharum*), native to eastern North America, was an important source of sugar for the Indians, and maple syrup is still much prized. Honey, perhaps the first sweet known to man, might also be considered a plant sugar in that bees manufacture it from the nectar of flowers.

## Sugar Cane

Although cotton is the plant most often associated with slavery in the United States, sugar cane was the plant most responsible for the establishment of slavery in the Americas. The need for labor to grow and harvest sugar cane in the West Indies led to the importation of large numbers of Africans at the beginning of the European colonization of the New World. Sugar cane very early became an important crop in tropical and subtropical America and today remains a major cash crop

*Figure 6–1* Sugar cane in flower, Costa Rica.

*Figure 6–2* Sugar cane for chewing, for sale in Mexico City.

*Figure 6–3*   Cutting sugar cane in Sri Lanka. (Courtesy of FAO.)

in many of the Latin countries, particularly Cuba and Brazil. In the United States it is grown in Hawaii as well as in some of the southern states.

Quite unlike the grasses treated in the last chapter, sugar cane (*Saccharum officinarum*) does not owe its importance to its seed and fruits. In fact, this grass, which is valued for its stem, often sets few or no seeds. In prehistoric times people found that by chewing the stem they could obtain a sweet juice, as they still do in many places. Domestication is thought to have occurred in New Guinea or Indonesia, and the plant spread throughout much of southeastern Asia. Europe learned of it through the travels of Alexander the Great when one of his men reported that in Asia the people were able to obtain honey without bees! Sugar cane did not become well known to the western world before the fifteenth century, and since that time it has spread throughout much of the world's tropics. Columbus is credited with having introduced it into the New World. Until the advent of the sugar-beet industry in the nineteenth century, sugar cane was the only source of sugar for most of the world's inhabitants, and today it still supplies over 50 percent of the world's sugar.

Sugar cane, a high polyploid species, is a tall plant, frequently reaching heights of 10 to 15 feet. Since it is a perennial, it will produce new stems for many years, but replanting is often done after the third harvest. Propagation is done vegetatively by using pieces of the stem. Extraction of the juice is accomplished by means of rollers. This is followed by purification that removes many of the "impurities," some of which are of nutritive value. The juice is then concentrated by evaporation. A boiling follows that leads to a crystallization yielding raw brown sugar and molasses. The brown sugar is then refined to produce white sugar. Except for the refining, all the steps in the processing of sugar are usually done on the plantation where the sugar is grown. The refining is frequently carried out in the importing countries of Europe or in the United States.

The refined sugar is one of the purest products to reach our tables and is one of our best energy sources. It has been said, however, that sugar contains "empty calories," by which is meant that it supplies us with nothing but pure carbohydrate. A diet consisting mostly of sugar can lead to malnutrition, as in the case of the "sugar babies" of the West Indies, who are fed mostly on sugar and suffer from protein deficiency as a result.

Sugar cane is said to give the highest yield of calories per acre of any plant, and more and more of this energy is being used to propel automobiles rather than humans. Alcohol can be made from biomass, such as wheat or potatoes or even crop residues or garbage. In the United States some "surplus" grain is being used to make alcohol for fuel, but some feel that to use grain for this purpose comes close to being immoral as long as there are hungry people in the world. Sugar cane, however, is not the basic staple that grain is. Moreover, overproduction has been a serious problem in many countries. Large amounts of sugar cane are used to make alcohol—*aguardiente* and rum— for human consumption. In 1975 Brazil launched an ambitious program to produce fuel alcohol from plants, particularly sugar cane, to reduce the need for expensive imported petroleum. Ethyl alcohol as fuel for automobiles is not new; it was first used in the last years of the nineteenth century, and for many years it has served as fuel for racing cars. As long as the price of gasoline remained low there was no incentive

*Figure 6–4*  Sugar beet. (Courtesy of USDA.)

to develop alcohol for wider use as a fuel. Even with the recent increases in the cost of gasoline it is still a cheaper fuel than alcohol. In fact, in the United States more energy is required to make a gallon of alcohol than it yields in return. However, as the price of gasoline continues to increase and methods of manufacturing alcohol from plants improve, the situation may change. Presently gasohol, a mixture of 10 percent alcohol and 90 percent gasoline, is being sold in this country.

## Sugar Beet

The beet (*Beta vulgaris*) is an ancient food plant of Europe, probably first used for its leaves like the modern variety known as Swiss chard, but its use for sugar production goes back only two centuries. In the eighteenth century it was recognized that the root of the beet contained sugar, and attempts were made to increase its sugar content. A plant

*Figure 6–5*   Quinua in the highlands of Ecuador.

breeder, Achard, received help from the King of Prussia for sugar-beet production, and the first processing plant was built in Selesia in 1801. In the early part of the nineteenth century Napoleon, in spite of ridicule, encouraged the new sugar-beet industry in France. He realized that it could give his country a domestic source of sugar, thus freeing it from dependence on England, which had a monopoly on sugar cane. The sugar beet, a biennial or annual, has since become a major crop in the north temperate zone. Sugar-beet growing became established in the United States in the latter part of the last century, and has become important in several states, notably Idaho, Colorado, and Michigan. Sugar content has been increased from the 2 percent of the ordinary beet to around 20 percent. Tetraploid varieties have been created but have not proved as satisfactory as diploid ones; however, triploids have been more successful and are now widely grown in Europe. In spite of mechanization of nearly all of the operations connected with sugar-beet growing and harvesting, beet sugar has difficulty competing with cane sugar, whose production still employs much cheap hand labor. Price supports from the government for beet sugar are necessary in the United States. There is no difference in the sugars of the two plants.

The beet is a member of the Chenopodiaceae, or goosefoot family. To the same family belongs the temperate zone vegetable spinach (*Spinacia oleracea*) of Old World origin, as well as quinua (*Chenopodium quinoa*), an old crop of the high Andes, where it is still grown. The seeds of quinua are used for thickening soups, for making a porridge, and sometimes for making *chicha*. Since quinoa is a good protein source, it is very important in the mountainous areas of the Andes, where the Irish potato and other starchy crops predominate among the food plants. Various wild species of *Chenopodium* known as lamb's-quarters, are collected in the United States for use as pot herbs.

# 7

# *The legumes:*
# *poor man's meat*

*And let them give us pulse to eat, and water to drink.*
Daniel 1:12.

The first cultivated plants in the Old World, as we have seen, were grasses—wheat and barley—but they were soon joined by plants that added valuable supplements to the diet—lentils, peas, and vetches, all members of the botanical family Leguminosae. From the archaeological record we know that people were collecting seeds from wild plants of these species at the time they were beginning to cultivate the grasses, and that their cultivation began not long after the domestication of the cereals. Cultivated lentils and peas appear in the archaeological record in the Near East nearly as early as wheat and barley. The evidence from the New World reveals that beans were among the first cultivated plants there, with two domesticated species appearing in Peru before 6000 BC, antedating the appearance of maize. In the Far East the soybean, destined to become more important perhaps than any other legume, became an early domesticated plant.

It can hardly be an accident that these plants were among the first domesticates in so much of the world, for their seeds are an excellent food and among the highest of all plant foods in protein content. Even though the cereals are given the credit for making civilization possible, it must be pointed out that it could not have advanced nearly as rapidly without the legumes. Not only are the legumes high in protein, but their amino acids neatly complement those of the cereals, as was explained in Chapter 3; if we eat legumes and cereals together we obtain a far more complete protein than from eating any plant food alone. Thus wheat plus peas, maize plus beans, or rice plus lentils come close to filling our protein needs. But in a way, the domestication of complementary food plants must be partly a "happy accident," for primitive people knew nothing of proteins or amino acids, only that the seeds satisfied their hunger.

A passage from the King James' Bible has been used to prove an early appreciation of the food value of the pulses, a name used for the edible-seeded legumes in England. After he was carried to Babylon, Daniel was ordered to eat the king's meat and wine. He resolved, however, not to defile himself by doing so and proposed a test. He and the servants would eat pulses and water while the other captive youths ate the king's meat and wine, and a comparison would be made at the end of ten days. At the end of that time, the Bible tells us, "their countenances appeared fairer and fatter than the children which did eat the portion of the king's meat." The argument for the value of the pulses loses its force, however, in modern translations of the Bible in which "meat" is given as "rich food" and "pulses" as "vegetables."

If we were to rank the families of plants in order of their importance to us, certainly the legumes would stand close to the grasses, for they serve not only as food but also perhaps in a greater variety of other ways than do the grasses. One of the greatest services they perform is the fixation of atmospheric nitrogen, that is, the conversion of this element to a form available to other plants. When plants and animals die and decay, their nitrogenous compounds are broken down by bacterial action. Some of the nitrogen released is made available to other plants in the form of nitrates, but much of it escapes to the atmosphere and is not directly available to plant life. Most members of the legume family, however, are able to obtain nitrogen from the atmosphere through the action of special bacteria that live in nodules on their roots. Very few other plants—no cultivated food plant among them—have this ability. Although the value of adding legumes to the soil had long been recognized, not until late in the nineteenth century was the scientific explanation for their importance discovered. The bacteria that live in the root nodules of legumes belong to several species of the genus *Rhizobium*; they derive their energy from their host plant and in turn provide nitrogen to the host in a symbiotic, or mutually beneficial, relationship. The fixed nitrogen goes into the production of protein,

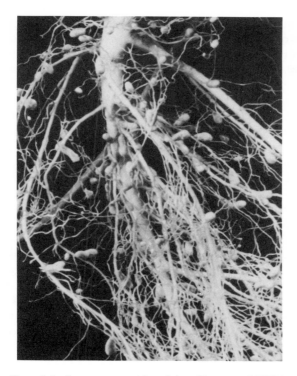

*Figure 7–1*  Legume root with nodules. (Courtesy of USDA.)

which is then available to humans through the seeds and to other animals through the leaves, stems, and seeds. When the plant dies, the nitrogen is returned to the soil, where it may be used by other plants. Although the nitrogen-fixing bacteria are widely distributed on wild and weedy legumes, farmers today, when planting a new field to legumes, often inoculate the seeds with a commercial preparation containing the bacteria, to insure the presence of nodules or to increase their abundance. Before commercial fertilizer was widely available, legumes were frequently employed in crop rotation schemes to build up soil fertility and they are still so used in many parts of the world.

The legume family is an extremely large and cosmopolitan one, and all the major continents have provided members of it that have become food plants. These plants are most commonly known by the names pulses, peas, or beans, but not all plants called beans belong to this family; castor bean, for example, is not a legume. The seeds are the part most commonly eaten, and like the cereal grains, most of them can be fairly readily stored for future use. Like the grasses, many of the domesticated legumes have lost their natural means of seed dispersal. Most members of the family produce a seed pod or fruit, called a legume, containing a row of seeds. In wild species the pod frequently is dehiscent at maturity, splitting along both sides, often forcefully expelling the seeds to some distance from the parent plant. Many of the domesticated forms have pods that are indehiscent*—an advantage to seed gatherers in that it makes it easy for them to collect all the seeds at the same time, but a disadvantage to the plant in that it interferes with the dispersal of seeds under natural conditions. The domesticated plants also have considerably larger seeds than their wild relatives, just as we saw for the fruits of the cereals.

The food value of the seeds is high; they have about the same caloric value per unit weight as cereals and are a fair source of some vitamins and minerals. However, as already mentioned, it is their protein content that is striking, generally ranging from 17 to 25 percent, about double that of most cereals, to a high of 38 percent in the soybean. The protein quality is not as good as that of meat and other animal products, but meat is not regularly available to much of the world's population. The legumes are thus often thought of as poor peoples' food, and many of the world's poor could use more of them. Consumption, as might be expected, is highest in India, where both poverty and religious restrictions on meat contribute to their great use, and it is also very high in Latin America, where beans are commonly served with all meals. A disadvantage to using the legumes for food is that many members of this family possess antidigestive factors. Many beans contain undigestable material that induces flatulence.

In addition to the seeds, the green, unripe pods of legumes are often consumed, green beans being one of the most common vegetables in the United States. Less well known is the fact that the ripe pods of several of the tree legumes have a high sugar content and are eaten by humans and livestock. People today still enjoy the pods of carob, or St. John's Bread (*Ceratonia siliqua*), native to Syria, for their sweet taste, although they use them mostly as livestock feed; these pods are the "locusts" of John the Baptist in the Bible. The sugar obtained from

---

*As a young professor of botany, I learned this the hard way. I brought green beans to class to illustrate the legume type of fruit, and I told my students that when they dried they would split open. They never did.

the pods is used in preparation of chocolate substitutes, including a candy bar that, according to the advertisements, tastes like fine Dutch chocolate. The genus *Inga* in Latin America has extremely large pods, some nearly a yard long, containing seeds covered with a sweet white pulp. The pulp is sucked or chewed off and the seeds discarded. This was one of the few sweets known to the people of this region until the introduction of sugar cane. The pods are sold in many markets in tropical America, and the trees are among the preferred species cultivated to shade coffee plants. Young sprouts or seedlings of various kinds of beans are a popular food in some places, particularly in the Far East. Several legumes have edible roots; one, *Pachyrrhizus*, the yam bean or jicama, is cultivated primarily for its root in parts of Latin America as well as in the Orient, where it was introduced.

Legumes rival grasses as foods for animals. When we speak of hay or forage, we generally are referring to both grasses and legumes, and sometimes to other plants as well. Leaves of legumes are particularly valuable for animals for the same reason that the seeds are for people— their high protein content. Alfalfa, or lucerne (*Medicago sativa*), is one of the best, since it is both high yielding and high in protein, and is probably the oldest cultivated forage plant. Seeds more than 6000 years old have been found in archaeological deposits in Persia. Alfalfa spread to Europe in early Christian times and in the last 150 years has made its way to most other parts of the world. Although it was introduced before the Revolutionary War, its importance as a crop in the United States dates from 1850, when seeds were brought to California from Chile by a gold miner. For a long time it was thought to be adapted only to the western states, but in this century varieties were found that would grow in other states, and now the north central states rival California in total tonnage produced. Alfalfa has been recommended as a human food and is sold by some "health food" stores, but it has never caught on—its flavor leaves something to be desired. Cigarettes made of alfalfa leaves have had the same fate and for the same reason.

Other important forage plants of the legume family include several species of clover, as well as lespedeza, kudzu, vetches, and some of the plants also grown for food, such as the field pea. Most of these plants are also of value in erosion control and soil building, and they provide food for wild life, including nectar for bees. Although perhaps not equal to the grasses in controlling soil loss, they may serve as better soil builders because of their ability to fix nitrogen.

The family has also furnished us with some of our favorite ornamentals, such as sweet peas, lupines, and scarlet runner beans among the herbs, the vine wisteria, and a great many trees—some grown for their flowers, some for their graceful leaves, others for both. In the temperate zone of the United States the native red bud and honey locust and the Asian *Albizia* are extensively cultivated. The tropics furnish a great many more, many of them with brilliant flowers, such as poinciana. Some mention must also be made here of *Mimosa*, the sensitive plant, native to tropical America but widely grown in greenhouses for its sensitive leaves, which close to the touch. Countless students of botany have seen this plant used to illustrate plant movements.

A number of the trees, particularly tropical species, are valuable sources of wood, one of them being the much prized rosewood. Other members of the family produce gums and resins that are used in medicine and in varnishes. Dye plants are also provided by the legumes; indigo, until replaced by synthetics, was particularly valuable. Flavorings such as licorice and tonka beans are still of some importance.

On the negative side, in addition to providing some weeds, the legume family also includes a number of poisonous plants, some of which have caused deaths in both humans and domesticated animals. A few of these deserve our attention. The jequirity bean, or rosary pea (*Abrus precatorius*), a woody vine that is rather widespread in the tropics, has been newsworthy on several occasions in recent years, with warnings appearing about the toxic effects of the seeds. Beads made from the attractive bright red and black seeds have been brought home by tourists or imported for sale by stores. They make beautiful necklaces, and are dangerous only if they are chewed and swallowed. The active principle, abrin, is one of the most toxic substances known, one seed containing enough to kill a person. It is reported, however, that in parts of Africa, the cooked seeds are eaten without harm! A few of the important leguminous food plants are known to be somewhat toxic under certain circumstances or to certain persons. The distinctive taste of the lima bean is due to a cyanide-containing compound, (cyanogenetic glucoside), and although beans grown and sold in the United States have only very small amounts of this substance, some varieties from the West Indies have enough to be considered dangerous.

Two diseases in humans, lathyrism and favism, are associated with legumes. The former results from consuming large amounts of the grass pea, or Indian pea (*Lathyrus sativus*). Eating the grass pea as part of an ordinary diet causes no harm, and the plant is in fairly wide use as food in both Asia and Europe. Difficulty usually arises when other food supplies are scarce and people are forced to subsist almost entirely

*Figure 7–2*  Novelty pins with jequirity beans used for eyes.

on the legume. As the grass pea does well on poor soil and withstands drought, it may be in plentiful supply when other foods are lacking. Excessive consumption of it leads to a paralysis of the lower limbs that may be permanent. The disease has been most severe in India, but it was known in ancient times from Europe. Favism, an acute anemic condition, results from eating the uncooked or only partially cooked broad bean (*Vicia faba*), also known as horse, Windsor, English, or fava bean, or from inhaling pollen from the plant. The disease affects only males of Mediterranean origin, and it is now thought that an inherited biochemical abnormality is responsible. Neither the grass pea nor the broad bean is eaten to any great extent in the United States.

The genus *Lupinus*, in addition to furnishing us ornamentals, has given us species used for food. Several species were domesticated in the Old World and one in the New for their seeds. Lupines contain alkaloids that are toxic, but inhabitants of the Old World selected alkaloid-free varieties for consumption by people and animals. One of these may be purchased at Italian markets in the United States under the name lupini bean. The Andean food species called *chocho* or *tarwi* (*Lupinus mutabilis*) however, does contain large amounts of a bitter alkaloid. To make the seeds palatable as well as safe to eat, they are soaked in water for several days, which leaches out the alkaloid. The *chocho* was once an important protein source in the high Andes in the area where the starchy potato was the major food source. Although it is still fairly commonly cultivated in parts of the Andes, it has been replaced in many areas by the broad bean, which also does well at high elevations and does not need the lengthy preparation prior to eating.

*Figure 7–3* Cultivated lupines *(Lupinus mutabilis)* in highland Ecuador.

Many of the wild plants in the family are also poisonous. Prominent among them are the locoweeds—various species of the genera *Astragalus* and *Oxytropis*—which are widespread in the western United States and which have been known to cause death in livestock that have grazed upon them. Although the family has supplied plants poisonous to humans, it has provided others that contain substances lethal to insects but relatively harmless to us. One of the safest insecticides, rotenone, comes from species of the South American genus *Lonchocarpus* and its Asiatic counterpart *Derris*. Long before their insecticidal properties were discovered, primitive people used these plants, as well as others, as fish poisons. The plants were pounded and placed in dammed-off waterways. The substance released from the plants stupified the fish, which were gathered as they came to the surface; the poisoned fish could be eaten without harm.

The list given here by no means exhausts all of the uses of members of the legume family, but it should serve to illustrate this plant family's broad significance. We may now return to some of the food plants and examine them in greater detail. Three of them, the common bean, soybean, and peanut, rank high among our most important domesticated species, and several others continue to occupy prominent roles as food plants.

As has already been pointed out, peas and lentils are among the very early cultivated plants of the Near East. They are still important there and throughout much of the world. The cultivated pea (*Pisum sativum*) comprises two main races or varieties—the field pea, now used mostly for forage and for dried peas, and the garden pea with its high sugar content, considered by some to be the aristocratic food plant of this family. Fresh peas were not popular before the seventeenth century, at which time they became esteemed in the court of Louis XIV. Whole pea pods used like green beans are a favorite food in the Far East, and are becoming increasingly popular in the United States. Biologists, of course, need no reminder that it was the pea that served as Mendel's research material for working out the laws of genetics.

The broad bean, previously discussed; chickpeas, or garbanzos (*Cicer arientinum*); and the cowpea, or black-eyed bean (*Vigna sinensis*) are other fairly important domesticates of Old World origin. The cowpea is widely used in the southern part of the United States. Another species, *Vigna sesquipedalis*, called asparagus, or yard-long, bean, is frequently offered by seed companies as a novelty, but those who grow it can hardly expect the beans to reach a yard in length. The specific epithet, translated as a foot and a half, comes closer to the truth.

No genus in the family has provided more edible species than has *Phaseolus*, and this is the group to which we generally refer when we speak of beans. Four different species were domesticated in the Americas. Two of these, the scarlet runner bean and the tepary bean, are of limited use today. The scarlet runner bean (*Phaseolus coccineus*) originally domesticated in Mexico, is grown in the United States mainly as an ornamental, but the large beans are a good food. The tepary bean (*Phaseolus acutifolius*), which was very important in prehistoric times in the American Southwest, is more drought resistant and less gas-forming than the other beans, but it is not grown commercially.

The lima, butter, or sieva, bean (*Phaseolus lunatus*) is fairly extensively cultivated today. This species was first domesticated in South America, and a large-seeded form is known archaeologically from Peru, dated at about 6000 BC. The earliest remains from Mexico are much later, about AD 800, and are small-seeded forms. The plant that may be the ancestral type, while not common, is fairly widely distributed in tropical America today, and it is thought that the large- and small-seeded types of lima beans may represent independent domestications. Although the lima beans in markets in the United States are nearly

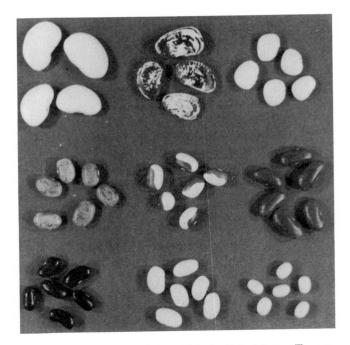

*Figure 7–4*  Some bean varieties sold in the United States. Top row: lima beans *(Phaseolus lunatus)*—Large Lima, Calico, Baby Lima. Bottom two rows: common beans *(Phaseolus vulgaris)*—middle row, Pinto, Yelloweye, Red Kidney; bottom row, Black Valentine, Great Northern, Small White.

always white when mature, a great variety of colors are known in those from Latin America. Speckled lima beans were used to convey messages in ancient Peru.

The most widespread and widely used bean today is *Phaseolus vulgaris*, known by a great variety of names, common bean, kidney bean, or simply, bean, being some of the most widely used in English. The snap, or green, beans and the wax beans are simply varieties of this species whose pod is eaten in the immature stage. This bean was domesticated in Peru before 6000 BC and in Mexico prior to 5000 BC. Its wild ancestral form is widespread in tropical America, and it seems likely that it was independently domesticated in Peru and Mexico. From Mexico it spread northward, as did corn and squash, and these three plants became the principal crops in North America in prehistoric times.

Today numerous varieties of the common bean are known; one estimate places the number at 500, only a few of which are grown in the United States. This bean is widely used in various parts of the world, and it still retains great importance in Latin America, where in different areas people have their own favorite varieties—red beans, or black beans, or other types. Mashed beans for breakfast are not uncommon in parts of Latin America and beans, as previously mentioned, may be served along with rice at every meal. Because the plants are vinelike, the Indians commonly planted beans among their maize plants so that they could use the stalks to climb on. Many beans are still grown this way but poles have replaced maize for supports in many areas. A mutant dwarf, or bush, type that needs no support has become a favorite in vegetable gardens in the United States.

The Old World beans formerly placed in the genus *Phaseolus* are now assigned to the genus *Vigna*. These include the black gram, or urd, bean; the golden gram, or mung bean; the adzuki bean; the rice bean; and the moth, or mat, bean. They are used mainly in India, China, Japan, and some of the neighboring areas. Their seeds are smaller than those of the American beans, and this may be one reason they have not been more widely adopted throughout the world. The germinated seeds of the mung bean are the widely used bean sprouts of Chinese cookery.

The two other legumes not yet discussed, the peanut and the soybean, are in many respects more significant than any of the foregoing, not only because of their exceptionally high protein content, but also for their high content of oils, which has given them numerous uses in industry as well as for food. The peanut (*Arachis hypogaea*), also called groundnut, groundpea, goober, pender, and many other names, is a rather unusual plant in that its fruits are produced under ground. The stalk of the flower elongates after fertilization and pushes the developing pod under the soil. The pod, or shell, is the fruit and the peanuts are the seeds.* For a long time it was thought that the peanut was indigenous to either China or Africa, but its true homeland is now clearly established to be South America. From there it was carried to other parts of the world in post-Columbian times. Its entry into the United States, however, was by way of Africa, for it was brought to Virginia by slaves. Archaeologically, the peanut is known from coastal Peru in

---

*Although they may be sold with the nuts at the grocery store, peanuts are not nuts, botanically speaking.

*Figure 7–5* Peanuts on freshly dug plant. (Courtesy of USDA.)

the second millennium BC, but recent botanical studies have indicated that the place of domestication was most likely the foothills of the Bolivian Andes. How early it was domesticated there and how it reached Peru pose interesting questions for the archaeologist and botanist.

Peanuts are reported in archaeological deposits in Mexico at Tehuahan in levels dated at about the beginning of the Christian era, but they never became as significant in Mexico as they did in parts of South America. The Mexican Indian name, *tlalcacahuatl*, means "ground cacao," presumably from the fruit being borne underground and its resemblance to the fruit of cacao, the chocolate plant. From this we get the modern Mexican name, *cacahuate*, although the word *mani*, which the Spanish picked up in the West Indies, is more widely used in other parts of Latin America.

Today the peanut, like its relative the soybean and many other crops—coffee, rubber, and quinine, for example—is grown more extensively in other parts of the world than in its place of origin. India and China lead the world in production of peanuts, followed by the United States and several African countries.* An attempt to grow peanuts on a huge scale in Africa led to one of the greatest agricultural fiascos in modern times. In 1946 the British government proposed to plant over 3 million acres of peanuts in East Africa for oil production. But clearing the land, irregular rainfall, and disease proved to be serious obstacles, and by 1951 only 65,000 acres were under cultivation. Later the project was abandoned, but only after over 100 million dollars had been spent. As John Purseglove has pointed out, this should be a lesson to those who would try to make abrupt changes in agricultural practice without sufficient research.

The peanut is put to far more uses in the United States than in any other part of the world. The plant is adapted to warm climates with light soil and is grown mainly in the southeastern part of the United States. It spread at a time when another crop was needed to replace cotton, which had been wiped out by the boll weevil. Only since 1850 has it become an important crop. In the last century most of the peanuts were used for roasting in the shell, and their prominence at circuses and baseball games can still be remembered. In fact, they were so much in demand that when one owner of a baseball park threatened to eliminate peanuts because of the work involved in cleaning up the shells, he almost had a rebellion on his hands. In the 1900s the mechanization of all operations connected with the growing and harvesting of peanuts was a strong impetus to increased production, and since that time peanuts have been a major crop in the United States. Of the numerous varieties of peanut only two, the Spanish and the Virginia, are commonly known in the United States.

The principal use of the peanut is for human food, and a protein content of 26 percent makes it an extremely valuable one. In the United States the greatest amount goes into peanut butter, and countless children, of course, have subsisted almost entirely on peanut butter sandwiches, often by choice. Although Indians of South America had long ago made a similar product, its use in the United States dates from

---

*A native African legume that also bears its fruit underground, the Bambara groundnut, was largely replaced by the peanut.

1890, when a physician in St. Louis came up with it in a search for a nutritious, easily digested food for invalids, and from 1893, when Dr. John Harvey Kellogg, the health-food faddist of breakfast-cereal fame, made peanut butter so that some of his patients with poor teeth could take advantage of what he called "the noble nut." Peanut butter is very simply made; the best grades are made by grinding the roasted and blanched nuts and adding one or two percent salt. Stabilizers are sometimes used so that the oil does not separate out. Considerable amounts of peanuts, some 70,000 tons annually, are also used in the manufacture of candy. Peanuts yield an oil that is esteemed as a cooking and salad oil and for the manufacture of margarine. There is considerable demand for peanuts in Europe, and in many years the United States produces a surplus that is used for export.

A cause of considerable concern in recent years has been the recognition that a mold infestation of peanuts produces aflatoxin, a harmful compound that may be carcinogenic. Fatalities are known to have occurred in animals from eating infected nuts. Since the aflatoxin can also be found in processed peanuts and other agricultural products, humans are also subject to poisoning. Fortunately, it is now recognized that by the use of proper harvesting and storage procedures, the fungus responsible for the aflatoxin can be eliminated.

George Washington Carver was instrumental in developing new uses for the peanut early in this century, realizing that the welfare of the South could be greatly influenced by this plant. Today peanuts are important industrially and are used in the manufacture of a number of products, from shaving creams to plastics. The residue from the oil-extraction process can be used for fertilizers and livestock food and could, with proper treatment, be used for human food. Peanuts are an excellent food for fattening hogs, and sometimes the animals are turned loose in the fields to root out the nuts for themselves. The shells can be used to make insulating filler and wallboard, as well as in other ways.

Although the peanut has come to be one of the world's important food plants, its rise to prominence hardly equals that of soybeans. The soybean (*Glycine max*) can hardly be considered a new crop. Although it didn't reach Europe before the eighteenth century and the United States until a century later, it was a very ancient and important cultivated plant in the Orient. Thus far there are no archaeological records to help us to establish when it was first cultivated, but its mention in Chinese literature before 1000 BC gives it a venerable age. The soybean is one of the richest foods known, containing 38 percent protein and

A

B

*Figure 7–6* A. Field of soybeans in the United States. (Courtesy of National Soybean Processors Association.) *B.* Soybeans ready for harvesting. (Courtesy of National Soybean Processors Association.)

18 percent fats and oils. Unlike most members of the legume family, the beans are seldom eaten directly but are used for food, it is said, in 400 different ways in the Orient. Paste, curd, and "milk" made from the beans are used in a great variety of ways, and the bean sprouts are used as a vegetable. Sauces of many different sorts are prepared by fermentation of the beans and addition of other ingredients such as salt and wheat; sometimes even decomposed chicken or fish is used, which further enriches the protein content of the food. A soft drink, Vitasoy, is now being made from soybeans in Hong Kong. Today China is a distant second to the United States in world production of soybeans. In recent years this legume has become an important crop in the temperate region of Brazil, which is now third in world production.

The widespread cultivation and utilization of soybeans in the United States in the space of a few decades must be one of the most spectacular success stories in the recent history of agriculture. Soybeans were first grown in the United States in Pennsylvania in 1804, and although at the time it was mentioned that they should be more extensively cultivated, very little was done until the 1920s. Five milllion bushels were produced in the United States in 1925. Production reached 13 million bushels in 1933, 90 million in 1939, 299 million in 1950, 699 million in 1963 and increased to 1080 million in 1968. Little wonder that it has been called the "Cinderella crop." A number of factors contributed to the crop's rapid growth. The introduction of more than 1000 strains from the Orient in the late twenties provided material for the selection of improved varieties for different parts of the country. It was found that the soybean was well adapted to the corn belt, where it now ranks as second only to maize.

Limits on the acreage of other crops by the government in the thirties encouraged the cultivation of the soybean. The development of specialized equipment for planting and harvesting was a factor in increased acreage being devoted to it, and the discovery that soybean meal was an excellent food for livestock, particularly poultry and hogs, made a large market readily available. At the same time, new food and industrial uses for the soybean came into being. Today the United States produces more than 60 percent of the world's soybeans, and about two-fifths of the crop is exported in one form or another, which makes it the United States' most important agricultural commodity in world trade.

Although it still has its greatest food use in the Orient, the plant has become increasingly used as food in other parts of the world, particularly as an additive for protein enrichment and as a meat substitute. By spinning the protein into long slender fibers and adding appropriate coloring, flavoring, and nutrients, soybeans can be made into synthetic beef, chicken, bacon, or ham. The taste, except possibly for the synthetic bacon, is not yet very close to the real thing, but improvements may be expected. The soybean is the world's greatest source of vegetable oil and the oil is of high quality. Most of it is used for the production of margarine, some for shortening and for salad and cooking oil. Soybean lecithin, a substance yielded in processing the oil, is used in many ways—to preserve flavors of other foods, to help disperse nonsoluble compounds in food, and in whipped toppings, cake mixes, and instant beverages. Eighty-five percent of the soybean crop in the United States goes into the production of food for humans and livestock, and the remainder finds many uses in industry, perhaps more than any other plant. It is used to make a glue that is the most widely used adhesive in binding plywood, and in the manufacture of enamels, linoleum, printing ink, and soaps—to name only a few.

Certainly many of the hungry nations could use this highly nutritious food but at present they get little or none of it. Although the soybean has been introduced into many tropical areas in this century, as yet it has met with little success in most of them. In some tropical areas of Africa where it is now grown the beans are used mostly for export, so it helps little in alleviating the local protein deficiencies.

# 8

# The starchy staples

*But don't forget the potatoes.*
John Tyler Pettee, *Prayer and Potatoes*

Cereals, as we have seen, are the basic food. However, in former times and even today, those who live in areas poorly adapted to growing cereals have had to adopt some other plant as the mainstay of their diet. Several of these plants—chiefly the potato, the sweet potato, the yam, manioc, and the banana—are still extremely important.

Although not closely related, all of them belonging to different botanical families, these plants have much in common. All are tropical in origin, although the potato comes from the highlands, whereas the others are lowland plants. They are all propagated vegetatively, rather than by seed. The archaeological record for most of them is scanty or nonexistent, as is true for most tropical plants, which grow in areas where conditions for preservation of plant remains are poor. All of them, with the exception of the banana, produce their edible parts underground. They provide extremely high yields of carbohydrates and thus they supply much energy and a full belly, but all are sadly deficient in protein. A diet made up almost exclusively of any of them can lead to serious problems of malnutrition.

## The Potato

The white potato (*Solanum tuberosum*), also known as the Irish potato, rivals maize in volume produced and in value. It had a long way to go before it became an acceptable food plant in Europe, but few plants have figured more prominently in Western history than has the potato. The story begins in South America. Wild potatoes are fairly widespread in the Americas, particularly in the Andes. They were probably found to be a valuable food when people first entered this area, and at some undetermined time, probably more than 4000 years ago, they came to be intentionally cultivated. With intentional selection there was an increase in size, and the potato became the most important food plant in the high Andes, for it thrives at an elevation where few other cultivated plants will grow. Maize will not grow at elevations much higher than 11,000 feet and is not a particularly productive plant at that altitude, but potatoes do well at 15,000 feet. Frost, common in parts of the Andes, is not conducive to keeping potatoes, but the Indians found a way to make it an ally. Potatoes were allowed to freeze at night, and the next day the Indians would stamp on the thawing potatoes. This process, repeated for several days, removes the water and results in a desiccated potato, called *chuño*, which may be kept almost indefinitely and used as required. Thus was born one of the original "freeze-dried" foods, in a sense the forerunner of instant mashed potatoes but with a somewhat different taste. Although the flavor of chuño is not pleasing to all foreign visitors in the Andes, it is still the staff of life to many Indians in highland Peru and Bolivia. The potato was cultivated throughout the length of the Andes in prehistoric times, but it did not make its way to Central America until it was introduced there by the Spanish.

The first European on record as seeing the potato in America thought that it was a strange food and compared it to the truffle. Potatoes were introduced into Europe in 1570 but their acceptance was far from immediate. The Jerusalem artichoke, introduced from North America at about the same time as the potato, was soon regarded as food fit for a queen; today it is seldom used for food, while the potato prevails. The slow acceptance of the potato was due to several factors. The newly introduced plant probably was not very productive at first, and the fact that it was recognized as a member of the nightshade family may have contributed to a reluctance to accept it. At this time the nightshade family was known in Europe mainly through its poisonous members—mandrake, henbane, and belladonna—and the family had not yet provided any important foods. Even after the potato gained some acceptance as food, there were many who disapproved of it. One minister preached against it, stating that if God had intended it as food for man it would have been mentioned in the Bible. Several writers of the time condemned it for its flatulent or "windie" property, among other rea-

*Figure 8–1* White, or Irish, potato plant. (From "The Late Blight of Potatoes" by John E. Niederhauser and William C. Cobb. Copyright © 1959 by Scientific American, Inc. All rights reserved.)

sons. At the start of the sixteenth century it was thought to be an aphrodisiac, a notion stemming from its confusion with the sweet potato, but this, of course, may have increased its use among some people. Promoted by royalty in some countries, the potato gradually became more widely grown. Various wars that destroyed standing crops of other food plants helped to increase its popularity, for the potato tubers, safe underground, could not be destroyed by burning as easily as a field of grain. The potato did not become really common in Europe before the eighteenth century, and there can be little doubt that it contributed to the increase of the population at that time, not because of any aphrodisiac property but because of its food value. World War I has even been blamed on the potato, since this food was responsible for the increased population that has been considered a contributing factor to the war. Certainly it was the potato that helped to keep Germany alive during two world wars.

In the early part of the nineteenth century the potato had become the dominant food in Ireland. In fact, it was almost the sole food of the peasantry, and the average consumption of potatoes was ten to twelve pounds per person a day. When a blight struck in 1845 and 1846, wiping out nearly the entire crop, famine followed. An estimated one and a half million people died as a result, and another million emigrated, many of them to the Americas. The blight disease was not understood at the time, and only later was it recognized that it was caused by a fungus. Since that time plant pathologists and breeders have devoted a great deal of effort to controlling the disease and developing resistant varieties. Much has been accomplished, but blight still causes serious losses in many parts of the world. It was formerly thought that eating blighted potatoes had no ill effect on humans, but recently it has been shown that a high incidence of certain kinds of birth defects characterizes areas where potato blight is common. In an experiment, marmosets who ate blighted potatoes as part of their ration produced some offspring showing birth defects; a control group of the animals, fed an ordinary diet, bore all healthy young.

Although the potato is often referred to as a root crop, the part eaten is actually an underground stem, specialized for food storage and known botanically as a tuber. The "eyes" of the potatoes are buds, and the so-called "seed potatoes" used for vegetative propagation are not seeds at all but portions of tubers, each containing an eye. Potato plants rarely flower in some northern areas, but they are capable of flowering and do so throughout much of their range. The attractive white, blue, or pink flowers produce small green berries, something like a small, unripe tomato, that contain seeds. Although these true seeds are not used by the farmer, they are important to plant breeders in creating new varieties. Vegetative reproduction, which is asexual, gives rise with rare exceptions to types exactly like the parent. Sexual reproduction by seed, on the other hand, allows for the production of new genetic combinations, some of which may be superior to the parents.

The potato tuber, like most vegetables, is mostly water; it contains 17 to 34 percent carbohydrate, small amounts of protein, a trace of fat, and some vitamin C. Varieties commonly cultivated in the north temperate zone contain from one to three percent protein, but some varieties grown in the Andes have six or seven percent. Although potatoes contain less protein than do cereals, they yield more than twice as many calories per acre than do wheat and rice. Many of the nutrients in the potato lie next to the skin; these are removed and therefore lost through the practice of deep peeling. The potato reveals its relationship to the other nightshades not only by its flower and fruit but also in that it may contain the toxic alkaloid solanine. Potato tubers grown exposed to light turn green and produce this alkaloid. Eating of the leaves or other green parts of the plants has caused poisoning in livestock and humans.

The English name *potato* for this plant is a mistake that goes back to the time of its introduction into England. The word potato is actually derived from *batata*, an American Indian name for the sweet potato. There was considerable confusion over the various new root crops being introduced into Europe in the sixteenth century, and the name of the sweet potato became attached to the white potato, where it remains.

Today nearly 300 million tons of potatoes are produced annually. About 70 percent of the production is in Europe, with the Soviet Union, Poland, and Germany being the most productive. In addition to their use as food for humans, large amounts of potatoes are fed to livestock in Europe, and some go into the production of starch, used chiefly for sizing cloth and paper. Potatoes also serve as a source of alcohol, both for drinking and for industrial purposes. The potato reached the United States from Europe by way of Bermuda in 1621, rather than directly from South America. In the United States today about eight million tons are grown for direct consumption and five million for use in other ways, much of that reaching the table as potato chips, frozen french fries, and dehydrated potatoes. A small amount is used for starch; the bulk of starch produced in the United States, however, is made from maize. The potato is, of course, still widely grown in the Andes, and in Mexico and Central America as well. It has been grown in India since the seventeenth century, and it later reached Africa, where it is now grown in the highlands, particularly in Kenya. It cannot be grown successfully in the lowland tropics, where its role as human food is taken over by some of the other starch crops, particularly manioc.

Along with the studies aimed at improving the potato, considerable study is also being given to its origin. The potato is a tetraploid species, and as yet there is no agreement as to what wild species were involved in its ancestry; many closely related wild species occur in the Andes. The suggestion has been made that it was first domesticated in the area of Lake Titicaca on the borders of Peru and Bolivia.

In the spring of 1970 five million pounds of potatoes were destroyed by fire in eastern Idaho. It was no accident, for the fire had been deliberately set by farmers in an attempt to raise the price. The same news report also carried the information that an estimated fifteen million Americans are underfed.

## Sweet Potato

At the time of the European discovery of the New World, the sweet potato (*Ipomoea batatas*) was widely cultivated in tropical America and was also being grown on some of the Pacific islands. In fact, the sweet potato had become the principal food of the Maoris in New Zealand. The presence of the plant on either side of the Pacific at such an early date poses several interesting questions—among them, how and when did it get across the ocean? The sweet potato is propagated vegetatively from stem cuttings or root sprouts. The plant under proper conditions may flower and set seeds, although, as with the white potato, seeds today are used only in breeding. It has been pointed out, however, that seeds, carried either by birds or on floating logs, may have reached the Pacific islands and given rise to plants that were later discovered and cultivated. The suggestion has also been made that the sweet potato might have been independently domesticated in the Americas and in the Pacific area from similar wild species. While either the introduction of seeds by some natural means or an independent domestication remains a possibility, it seems far more likely that people were responsible for the introduction of the sweet potato from the Americas to the Pacific region. There are two ways in which this might have occurred.

Ancient Polynesian voyagers, who were efficient seamen, could have traveled to South America and picked up sweet potatoes, then carried them home and cultivated them. Or, and perhaps more likely, Peruvians, who also are known to have had seaworthy vessels, may have carried the sweet potato to one of the Polynesian islands, not necessarily intentionally but perhaps when driven off their normal course by winds.

*Figure 8–2*   Sweet potatoes on vine.

The prevailing currents are in the right direction for such a trip, and there is no need in this case to account for a return voyage. There may be some question about whether the sweet potatoes would not have been eaten on the journey and, if not, whether they still would have been viable after such a long voyage, for sweet potatoes are rather perishable.

The presence of the sweet potato in both the Pacific region and South America does not necessarily mean that voyages across the Pacific were frequent in prehistoric times. If they had been, we would expect other plants to have been exchanged among the peoples of the two areas. Many such claims have been made for the spread of other plants, but except for two of them the evidence is unconvincing. The only plants besides the sweet potato that did become established on both sides of the Pacific in prehistoric times are the coconut and the bottle gourd, both of which have fruits that float and hence are well adapted to dispersal by ocean currents. The voyage of the *Kon Tiki* by Thor Heyerdahl was an attempt to prove that primitive people could have crossed the Pacific successfully, and Heyerdahl and others have claimed that there were significant contacts in prehistoric times, with an exchange of cultivated plants. There may have been such voyages, but so far as plants are concerned, the only support for the idea of exchange appears to be provided by the sweet potato, and a single accidental voyage could account for that.

Although the origin of the sweet potato has recently received considerable attention, much of its early history in the Americas remains obscure. The sweet potato, like bread wheat, is a hexaploid. An allegedly wild species, *Ipomoea trifida*, also a hexaploid, has recently been reported from Mexico and is considered by Ichizo Nishiyama to be the ancestor of the domesticated plant. If this is true, it would seem likely that the sweet potato had its origin in Mexico. However, some botanists feel that *Ipomoea trifida* is an escaped form of the domesticated sweet potato and not a truly wild plant. The lack of popularity of the sweet potato in Mexico suggests that it may have originated elsewhere, and anthropological and linguistic considerations indicate that this may have been in northwestern South America. In this connection it is of interest that archaeological remains of the sweet potato are known from Peru but have yet to be found in other areas. The plant was being grown in the Caribbean area as well as in mainland America when the Spanish arrived. The exact place or places of its origin as well as the history of its dispersal remains to be clarified.

The post-Columbian history of the sweet potato, as is to be expected, is much better known. Columbus took the plant to Spain, and it later became a common staple on ships on return voyages to that country. The Spanish also introduced it from Mexico to Guam so that it might be available for ships' supplies on voyages to the Far East. As the plant is adapted to warm climates, it was not cultivated in most of Europe. Sweet potatoes grown in Spain were imported into England, where for reasons not entirely clear they were regarded as an aphrodisiac. Humankind has always wanted to attach aphrodisiacal properties to plants, and it is only natural that such properties would become associated with exotic plants instead of those already well known.

The plant had various names in the Americas—*apichu* among the Quechua of Peru, *camote* in Mexico, and *aje* for starchy types and *batata* for sweet types in the Caribbean area.* Of these, the last became the

---

*The name *kumar*, or variants of it, was used in both Peru and Polynesia for the sweet potato. Until recently it was claimed that this was further evidence that the sweet potato was introduced from Peru to the Pacific area, for it would be most unlikely for the same name to have been independently chosen in the two areas. The Peruvian origin of the name has been questioned in recent years, and it has been postulated that *kumar* was actually of Polynesian origin and was introduced into Peru in the early post-Columbian period.

most generally accepted and was transferred to the white potato as related above, so that we now have to refer to the plant under discussion as the sweet potato. This name, of course, is not inappropriate, since three to six percent of the carbohydrate is in the form of sugar, and the amount may increase in storage and with cooking. The plant provides 50 percent more calories than the white potato, but generally has less protein (one and a half to two percent). It is a good source of vitamin A and of minerals. In contrast to the white potato, the part eaten is a true root.

Although the sweet potato is still widely grown in the Americas and has become an important crop in the southern United States, it is now more extensively cultivated in Africa and southeastern Asia. Although its importance in Japan has declined in recent years, that country still produces twice as much as the United States. In addition to its use for human and livestock food, considerable amounts are used for alcohol production in Japan. In both Japan and Taiwan, the crop is regarded as "typhoon insurance," for when rice and other standing crops are destroyed the sweet potatoes will still be available for food.

The sweet potato is a member of the morning-glory family. The flowers, seldom if ever produced under temperate-zone conditions, bear a close resemblance to the ornamental forms of the morning glory. Although more common at lower elevations, the plant can be success-fully cultivated as high as 9000 feet in the tropics. The roots cannot stand waterlogging, and for this reason the plants are often grown on ridges or mounds to provide good drainage. The vines rapidly cover the ground and hence the plants require little cultivation. In spite of the fact that for agricultural production the crop requires good drainage, the roots will sprout readily if placed in a jar of water, and the vines will grow luxuriantly; not infrequently such plants are grown as or-namentals in the home. In some areas the leaves as well as the roots have served as food.

## Manioc

Manioc, cassava, and yuca* are some of the common names of *Manihot esculenta*. This plant is little known to most people in the temperate zones except in the form of tapioca, although it is one of the extremely

---

*Not to be confused with *Yucca*, an entirely different plant.

*Figure 8–3*   Manioc plantation, Ecuador. (Courtesy of FAO.)

important food plants of the tropics of both hemispheres. Although manioc is New World in origin, details about where and when it was first domesticated remain vague. Related wild species occur in both South and Middle America. Prehistoric remains are known from coastal Peru, but it is generally agreed that manioc was introduced there, perhaps from Venezuela or Brazil. The plant may have been independently domesticated in Middle America, but an introduction from South America to Middle America seems more likely. Manioc belongs to the Euphorbiaceae, or spurge family, which includes, among many other plants, the Pará rubber tree, our best source of natural rubber, and the poinsettia, a well-known Christmas ornamental. The manioc plant is rather tall, at times reaching fifteen feet, with divided leaves. The edible part is the tuberous root, which somewhat resembles a sweet potato but is usually much larger—some grow to be a yard long and to weigh several pounds. Numerous rather ill-defined varieties exist that are generally divided into two groups, the sweet maniocs and the bitter. The latter contain higher concentrations of poisonous cyanide compounds (cyanogenetic glucosides) than the former and require special preparation by grating, pressure, and heat to make them safe to eat. One wonders, of course, how anyone discovered that this plant, as well as several others that are toxic until specially prepared could be made edible.

Manioc was taken to Africa from Brazil by the Portuguese in the sixteenth century, but it did not spread widely there until the twentieth century, when its cultivation was encouraged. It was found that manioc was not damaged by locusts, a serious pest of crops in many parts of Africa, and that the bitter varieties could be grown in areas where wild animals would destroy other crops. The plant also grows better on poor soil than any other major food plant. As a result, Africa today produces as much as or more than the rest of the world combined, which in one sense is unfortunate, since the roots contain little protein and their wide use has contributed to malnutrition. The plant reached the eastern tropics somewhat later than Africa, and presently is most important in Indonesia, where it ranks as the third most important crop, after rice and maize. Some is grown there for export, but most of it is used locally for food, as is true in most other areas where the plant is grown. World production is estimated at more than 110 million tons.

Manioc is a lowland tropical crop, although sometimes it is grown at elevations as high as 6000 feet. It will grow in somewhat arid regions as well as in regions with fairly high rainfall. Stem cuttings are used for propagation; these are simply stuck in the ground at an angle in fields prepared by slashing and burning. The plants are then more or less left to themselves. In some varieties the roots mature in as little as six or seven months, and in others roots may continue to increase in size for up to four years. The roots are harvested as needed at the farmer's convenience. The plants are extremely productive.

The peeled roots of the sweet types of manioc may be prepared for eating simply by boiling or roasting. Both sweet and bitter varieties may be used to yield a coarse meal, known as *farinha de mandioca* in Brazil. The meal is often prepared by placing cut roots into a long sleevelike basket, known as *tipiti* in Brazil. The *tipiti*, which works something like a Chinese finger lock, is tied to a tree and pressure is exerted on the other end. The pressure extracts the juice, which is also collected and is often used to prepare sauces or beers. Among some Indians in the lowland regions of tropical South America, the beer is prepared by old women who sit around a large gourd vessel, chew the roots, then spit them into the gourd. The chewing initiates a breakdown of the starch into sugar, and wild yeasts then take over the production of alcohol. Visitors to a tribe are often expected to take a ritual drink of the beer, and to refuse to do so would be considered an insult.

At one time manioc was in demand in the United States in the form of tapioca. Once a popular pudding, tapioca has been largely replaced

*Figure 8–4* Expressing hydrocyanic acid from grated manioc with a *tipiti*.

by gelatins and instant puddings. The fact that some people referred to tapioca pudding as "fish eyes," a fairly apt description, probably did not figure in its decline. Tapioca, as purchased for making desserts, is prepared by gentle heating, the partial cooking causing the agglutination of the manioc starch into small pellets. In addition to its use as food, manioc starch is used in the manufacture of adhesives and cosmetics, for sizing textiles, and in making paper. Since many of its former uses have now been taken over by starch from waxy maize, little manioc now enters into international trade.

In some places, particularly in Africa, manioc leaves are used as a pot herb. Since the leaves may contain up to 30 percent protein, their wider use might help prevent malnutrition among manioc-root eaters. One of the aims in present manioc improvement programs, which unfortunately are being conducted only on a very small scale, has been an attempt to increase protein content. Most varieties have one percent protein or even less in the roots, but a few have been reported to have nearly three percent, although these high protein types produce small, somewhat woody roots. Hybrids have been made in hope of transferring the trait of higher protein content to more productive varieties. Attempts are also underway to produce types low in cyanogenetic glucosides, and some success has already been achieved in breeding for resistance to a virus that has caused considerable loss in Africa.

## Yams

In prehistoric times the most widely distributed of the starchy crops were the yams, various species of the genus *Dioscorea*. There is no need to call upon man as an agent for their very wide dispersal, for the genus contains some 600 species, native to the tropics of both hemispheres. People in many different areas discovered independently that the large underground stems, or tubers, were a good source of food. The tubers of some species under cultivation may reach a remarkable size, six to nine feet long and weighing more than 100 pounds.

The true yams are largely confined to the tropics and are little known in the United States. Most of the so-called "yams" in markets in the United States are moist-fleshed varieties of sweet potatoes. One true yam species, *Dioscorea bulbifera*, is sometimes cultivated in greenhouses under the name "aerial potato" or "yam potato." The small aerial tubers, or bulbils, produced on this vine are sometimes used as food in parts of Asia and Africa.

Yams grow best in humid and semihumid regions. They are usually grown on a small scale by farmers for their own use, frequently in shifting cultivation, so that new fields are sought after a few years. Tuber cuttings, small tubers, or bulbils are used for planting. The plants are usually grown in ridges or mounds, and stakes are often provided as supports for the vines. The harvest season, which is an important occasion to those people for whom this plant is the major food source, is celebrated with special rites. After harvest, the tubers are stored; they are later boiled, roasted, or fried as they are needed.

Today the greatest production is in West Africa, where in many places the yam is the principal food plant, as it is in parts of southeastern Asia, which is second in production. Large quantities of yams are also still cultivated in the Caribbean. The species introduced from the Old World, which first came to America as food supplies in slave ships, are now probably more extensively cultivated in the West Indies than is the native American plant.

A

B

*Figure 8-5*   *A*. Greenhouse plant of potato yam *(Dioscorea bulbifera)* showing the aerial "potatoes," or tubers. *B*. Tubers of *Dioscorea alata*. Some tubers of this yam grow to be several feet long. (Courtesy of USDA.)

Yams, however, are no longer as important in the Old World as they once were, chiefly because of the introduction of other tuber crops, particularly manioc. In one sense this is unfortunate, for yams have a higher protein content than has manioc. On the other hand, the large amount of manual labor required to grow yams makes the crop a relatively inefficient one in terms of food yield for the manhours spent on it. Little work has been done in an attempt to improve the yam, chiefly because it is a crop that is consumed locally and does not enter into trade with the developed nations. The cultivated plants are little used except as a source of food.

Some of the wild yam species have also been used as food in periods of famine by some people in the tropics. Many of the wild species, however, contain toxic substances and require special treatment to make them safe to eat. They have been known to cause deaths in humans. It is some of these same toxic substances, however, that have made the wild species useful in some other ways. Some of them have been used as fish poisons, similar to the way rotenone is used, and around 1940 some steroids in *Dioscorea* were found useful in the manufacture of cortisone and sex hormones. At one time the steroids useful in the treatment of Addison's disease, asthma, arthritis, and skin diseases, were thought to occur only in animals, and their production was very expensive. As a result of the discovery of plant sources, the cost of hormones fell from $80 a gram to $2 in ten years. A still more significant use became known in 1956, when Dr. Gregory Pincus announced that a drug derived indirectly from *Dioscorea* would stop ovulation and hence prevent conception. Up to that time, steroids that prevented conception had to be taken by injection, whereas it now became possible to use oral administration. Tests of the new drug in Puerto Rico and Los Angeles were successful, and the birth-control pill was on its way. Although most birth-control pills are wholly synthetic today, *Dioscorea* still figures in their origin, and in this way the plant has contributed more to controlling the world hunger problem than it will ever do as a food.

## Taro

Another tropical crop that feeds millions of people is taro, or dasheen. It was probably originally domesticated in southeastern Asia, although our earliest historical record comes from China. Details about its origin have not yet been worked out, but it is known to have been carried quite early from its homeland to Japan. It was also introduced into the Pacific islands, apparently by Polynesians, and there it is still a staple in some areas. Taro eventually reached Africa and was carried from there by slaves to tropical America. It was introduced into the southern United States in 1910 as a crop in soils too moist for potatoes, but it never made much impact, for it couldn't be grown economically enough to compete with other root crops.

Taro (*Colocasia esculenta*) is very similar in appearance to elephant's-ear, a plant grown as an ornamental or a curiosity for its extremely large heart-shaped leaves. These plants belong to the Araceae, or aroid family, which perhaps is best known to most Americans through *Philodendron*, widely grown as a house plant. Members of this family usually contain crystals of calcium oxalate in nearly all parts of the plant, and these can be toxic. Anyone who has ever bitten into the tuber of Jack-in-the-pulpit, another member of this family, is familiar with the action of these crystals. The effect might be compared to biting into a pincushion with pins present. Fortunately, the calcium oxalate crystals are usually destroyed by boiling. The American counterpart of taro is yautia, that is, any of various species of *Xanthosoma*, an ancient cultivated plant, and both it and taro are cultivated in parts of lowland tropical America today.

Leaves of taro are eaten, but the part usually consumed is the underground portion, known as a corm and made up mostly of stem tissue. The corms contain about 30 percent starch, three percent sugar, and a little more than one percent protein; they are fairly good sources of calcium and phosphorus. Reportedly, thousands of varieties are known, with the flesh color of the corms ranging from white to yellow and pink. A pink-fleshed variety, which is one of the favorites today, reputedly was reserved for royalty in early times in Hawaii. One of the favorite methods of use in Hawaii, then as now, was to make poi. Steamed corms are crushed, made into a dough, and allowed to ferment for a few days. The dough is then eaten by dipping into it with the fingers or rolling it into small balls. In Hawaii people used to eat 10 to 20 pounds of poi a day, to which some have attributed the traditional obesity of the Hawaiian people, a trait greatly admired among themselves. Commercial preparation is now carried out and has largely replaced the making of poi at home. Not all visitors to the Islands find poi an acceptable food, some comparing the taste to library paste.

The Hawaiian luau gets its name from the leaves of taro, which are used as part of the meal. The leaves are a good source of vitamins A and C and undoubtedly contain considerably more protein than the corms. The leaf stalks are a favorite food in much of Polynesia. A taro

A

B

*Figure 8–6*   *A*. Taro plants. (Courtesy of Hawaii Visitors Bureau.) *B*. Taro corms. (Courtesy of USDA.)

flour, taro chips, and breakfast foods have been made from the corms in Hawaii. Since taro is easily digested, it has been recommended for use in baby foods. Today, however, there is little use of processed taro outside of Hawaii.

Taro is one of the few important cultivated plants that thrive in wet soil, although certain varieties can grow in relatively dry areas. The ancient Hawaiians accomplished some rather remarkable engineering feats to provide suitable areas for its cultivation. The propagation is vegetative, from corm tops or axillary corms, since the plant rarely flowers and seldom sets seed. The statement may sometimes be seen in older books that the plant has been in cultivation so long that it no longer flowers. Although the exact cause of the failure to flower is not known, age almost certainly has nothing to do with it. It more likely reflects a hybrid origin, mutations, or the fact that the plants are cultivated in areas where the day during the growing season is of an improper length to induce flowering.

## Breadfruit

Another plant that has served as a staple, although not as important as any of those already discussed, is the breadfruit (*Artocarpus altilis*), a member of the Moraceae, or mulberry family. The breadfruit is a handsome tree, 40 to 60 feet tall, with shiny, deeply lobed leaves. The large fruits in reality are multiple fruits, since each develops from the ovaries of a tight cluster of flowers rather than from a single flower. Sometimes reaching a foot in diameter and ten pounds in weight, the fruits are a rich source of carbohydrates, and have been used as a food in Polynesia since prehistoric times.

Captain James Cook saw the tree in his voyages in the Pacific, and from his descriptions some Englishmen thought that breadfruit would make a wonderful food for slaves in the West Indies. Captain William Bligh, who had sailed with Cook, was commissioned to bring trees to the West Indies from Tahiti. Thus began the famous voyage of the H.M.S. *Bounty* in 1789. The ship left Tahiti with more than 1000 young trees, but as a result of the mutiny led by Fletcher Christian, they never reached their destination. The exact cause of the mutiny is not completely clear to this day. Some have held that Captain Bligh's behavior was responsible; others, including Bligh, have thought the attractive native women may have played a role. Some of the mutineers did remain in Polynesia and married local women. Captain Bligh and

*Figure 8–7* Breadfruit tree. (Courtesy of Hawaii Visitors Bureau.)

18 faithful sailors were put on board a small boat and a month and a half later arrived safely at Timor. In 1792 Bligh remade the journey and this time did manage to transport trees to the West Indies. Such a story obviously should end with the breadfruit becoming an important food plant in the West Indies, but it never did. The West Indian blacks did not eagerly adopt it, much preferring bananas and plantains and other foods already familiar to them. But as a testimony to Captain Bligh's persistence, the breadfruit is now well established in tropical America, the trees being appreciated for their ornamental value and occasionally used for food. Captain Bligh has been honored by having another tree named after him, *Blighia sapida*, the akee; its fruit is edible, but if eaten when unripe or overly ripe it can cause death.

*Figure 8–8* Jackfruit. (Courtesy of USDA.)

Both seedless and seeded forms of breadfruit are known. Seedless breadfruit is generally prepared by boiling or baking. The seeded type is grown primarily for its seeds, called breadnuts, which are cooked and eaten. In parts of the Pacific area a cloth is made from the fibrous inner bark of the breadfruit tree. The details of the domestication of the breadfruit are unknown, but it has been suggested that the cultivated plant is of hybrid origin. The seedless forms obviously represent variants selected by man, since they cannot propagate naturally.

The genus *Artocarpus* also contains another species grown for its edible fruits and seeds. The jackfruit (*Artocarpus heterophyllus*) is native to the Malay region and widely distributed in the tropics today, although of less importance than the breadfruit. It, too, is an attractive tree, differing from the breadfruit in having entire rather than lobed leaves and much larger, sweeter fruit. The fruit, which is reported at times to reach lengths of nearly three feet and weights of more than 75 pounds, has been stated to be the largest fruit of any cultivated plant. It may well be the largest fruit of any cultivated tree but there are pumpkins and squashes on record that far exceed it in size and weight. Moreover, these latter fruits each develop from the ovary of a single flower, whereas the fruit of jackfruit, like that of breadfruit, is made up of the ovaries from many individual flowers.

## Bananas

Many people who think of the banana only as a dessert fruit may be surprised to find it included with the staples. In many parts of the tropics, particularly in East Africa, it is the principal food of various peoples. Of the 37 million tons of bananas produced annually, only about 15 percent enters the world trade, the remainder being consumed locally. About one-half of the bananas are eaten raw in the way familiar to us, and about one-half are eaten cooked, as a vegetable. The dessert, or sweet, banana is sometimes cooked, but most cooking bananas are starchy rather than sweet and are referred to as plantains or cooking bananas.

The bananas had their origin in southeastern Asia, many in the Malay region. Our earliest record is an account from India in 500 BC, but it is generally assumed that the banana is a much more ancient crop, although its exact age is unknown. Wild bananas have relatively small fruits with many hard seeds and probably were not a particularly attractive food. Other parts of the wild plants may have been eaten more frequently—the large underground part, or corm, the shoots, and the large male bud—as they still are in some places in the tropics. The leaf stalk also may have been used for its fibers. Thus, other parts of the plant were probably much more important to early people until there was a genetic change that led to seedless fruits. The discovery of such a plant was fortunate: the banana became more useful, and because it now had to depend upon man for its spread, there was selection for increased size and improved flavor as time went on. Seedlessness in bananas derives from both parthenocarpy, or the development of fruit without pollination, and sterility. The species that is ancestral to our domesticated bananas is *Musa acuminata*, which still exists in the form of numerous races in southeastern Asia. At some time this species hybridized with another, *Musa balbisiana;* today some of our cultivated bananas are "pure" *Musa acuminata* and others contain one or two chromosome sets from *Musa balbisiana.* An important event in the development of the edible bananas was the addition of a chromosome set to the normal diploid set. Such triploids, derived from crosses of diploids and tetraploids, are more productive and vigorous than diploid bananas and are also usually sterile and quite variable, giving us some superior plants to choose from. Today most of our bananas are triploids, although some diploids and a few tetraploids are cultivated.

The banana reached Africa at about the beginning of the Christian era, along with several other food plants from southeastern Asia. Some have thought that the introduction of these plants led to a population explosion in Africa at this time. The plant was first heard of in Europe from a report of Alexander the Great, and Pliny wrote that it was the plant of wise men—hence one of Linnaeus' names for the banana, *Musa sapientum,* "of the wise men." Another Linnaean name formerly used was *Musa paradisiaca,* for the plant was thought to have been regarded as the Tree of Paradise or the Tree of Knowledge among some people. From Africa the banana was carried to the Americas in 1516 and became so well established in a short space of time that some early travelers thought that it was an indigenous American plant. From Africa, too, came the name *banana.*

The modern history of bananas began in the last half of the past century, when schooners began carrying bananas from Central America to the United States. One of the most significant events occurred in 1871 when a railroad was built in Costa Rica. Looking for something for his railroad to carry, the builder, American magnate Minor Cooper Keith, began banana plantings in that country three years later. In 1899 the Keith interests and the Boston Fruit Company merged to form the United Fruit Company, which was to become dominant in the banana industry. In the first years of this century refrigerated ships began to operate, and bananas started to come to the United States with some regularity. We now import more bananas than any other country; half of all world exports go to the United States, most of them coming from Central America. In the early years Honduras and Costa Rica were among the world's leading exporters, but when a fungus disease destroyed many of the commercial plantings in Central America, the small South American republic of Ecuador became the world's chief exporter, a position that it continued to hold until recently. The Central American countries are now growing varieties resistant to disease; although many people do not find the flavor of these bananas as pleasing

*Figure 8-9* Bananas. The pointed structure at the tip of the bunch (bottom) is the male bud. (Courtesy of USDA.)

as that of the older variety, these countries now supply most of the export trade, and Ecuador has lost its former position. Since bananas had become the principal export crop of Ecuador, its whole economy was threatened when this change occurred.*

The banana not only comes in one of the neatest and most convenient packages of all of our food plants, but is also one of our best energy

---

*Since some have pointed out that cereals were stored in granaries in the United States while much of the world went hungry, it might also be mentioned that bananas have been known to rot in coastal Ecuador while some people in the highlands of the country went hungry. Similar examples could be drawn from many countries.

sources. Its nutritive value is very similar to that of the white potato, although in the dessert varieties more of the carbohydrate is in the form of sugar. The average person would need to eat about 24 bananas a day if they were his sole source of calories. Bananas contain considerable amounts of a substance called serotonin that may be slightly poisonous, and Pirie has written that "dependence on them as the main source of energy would be inadvisable." But in parts of the world people do use them as their principal food source.

The banana plant, contrary to popular notion, is not a tree. The trunk of the banana is not woody and is not even a stem, but consists of the leaf stalks. It also may surprise some people to learn that the fruit is classed as a berry. The plant is a perennial herb, the aerial portions arising from a corm. The pseudostem produces a bunch of bananas and then is removed or eventually dies naturally, but side-shoots, or suckers, from the same corm continue to grow, and stems from these will produce bunches of bananas in the following seasons. Suckers or corms are used for propagation. In a sense the plant is immortal, although in practice most banana plantations are started anew after 5 to 20 years. Some, however, have been known to remain in production for up to a hundred years.

The banana is for the most part a tropical crop. It needs considerable warmth and water, with adequate drainage. Some bananas, however, are produced in relatively dry subtropical areas, usually under irrigation. The plant needs little attention other than pruning to remove unwanted suckers. It is fairly taxing of the soil, and clean cultivation, or removal of all weeds in the plantation, which tends to promote erosion, is no longer recommended.

Only a very few of the some 300 varieties of bananas ever reach the United States, and by far the most common in the past was the variety Gros Michel. The varieties known as Valery and Cavendish, more resistant to some diseases, have now largely replaced it. Other varieties are known that are better tasting, but unfortunately they don't ship as well as those previously named. Bananas are cut while quite green, even for local use in the tropics, where the sweet types are allowed to ripen in a shady place near the house to be used as needed. Fruit intended for export is ripened under carefully controlled conditions and ethylene is sometimes used to hasten the process.

Although more than 90 percent of the bananas grown are used directly for food, several products are made from the remainder. A banana flour or powder is sometimes produced. According to the primitive

*Figure 8–10* Harvesting abaca. The trunk, which is made up of the leaf stalks, is used for its fiber. (Courtesy USDA.)

method of drying the fruits for flour, the bananas were placed in heaps on mats over a mixture of cow dung and water and covered with leaves. Modern methods involve slicing the bananas and drying them by artificial means. Candies and various confections are made by splitting and drying the bananas. Sliced dried bananas are used as banana chips. A beer for local consumption is made from bananas in parts of Africa. Other parts of the plant are sometimes used for food. The leaves are often employed for wrapping—the thick, waxy covering of the leaf makes it an ideal "wax paper"—or for plates, and at times for emergency umbrellas.

The leaf fiber of the banana is of no commercial importance, but members of other species of the same genus have valuable fibers. *Musa textilis*, commonly known as abaca, or Manila hemp, looks very much like a banana but has an inedible fruit; it produces a very strong fiber in the leaf stalk that is used to make high grade cordage. The fiber is one of the principal exports of the Philippines. The plant became well established in tropical America during World War II and was grown widely in Central America on banana plantations devastated by disease.

Scientific breeding work with the banana has been carried out for only half a century, nearly all of it in Trinidad. Much of the early work was necessarily concerned with learning as much as possible about the plant. Seeds are required for breeding work, and fortunately most edible bananas will produce seeds, although in very small numbers, if pollinated. Only a start has been made in an attempt to breed new, improved varieties.

# 9

# The coconut:
# the most useful tree

*No part of the coconut tree is wasted.*
Malayalam proverb

Although most people in the temperate zone are aware that palms are graceful, attractive trees of the tropics, few realize their great usefulness. In fact, many botanists consider the palm family (Palmae) second only to the grass family in its importance to humankind, and in many parts of the tropics palms are far more important than are the grasses. There are more than 2000 species of palms, and a long list of useful ones could be given that would certainly include the coconut, the date palm, the African oil palm, the rattan palm, the wax palm—carnauba, the world's preferred wax, comes from a palm—and the sago palm,* whose stem yields a starchy food used in Malaysia and Indonesia.

The date palm (*Phoenix dactylifera*) has been considered the "tree of life" in the subtropical deserts of the Old World and was a symbol of fecundity and fertility. Its fruit has long served nomadic Arabs as a staple food. In addition to its high sugar content (about 70 percent),

---

*A number of plants share the common name sago palm, including several different species of the palm family; however, some plants known by this name are not members of the family.

*Figure 9–1*   Date palm in fruit, California.

the date contains about two percent protein and two percent fats, and is a fair source of some vitamins and minerals; it thus is a considerably better food than are some of the starch crops. Like most palms, the date palm has many other uses—360 of them according to an ancient Persian source. Although the date palm is widely used, the coconut (*Cocos nucifera*) is nevertheless the world's most important palm. Today the demand for its oil is not as great as it once was, but the coconut continues to serve people in many ways.

In addition to having been called "man's most useful tree," the coconut has also been referred to as "one of Nature's greatest gifts to man" and "mankind's greatest provider in the tropics." People use practically all parts of the plant in one way or another, but it is the fruit (botanically classed as a drupe, not a nut) that gives the plant its great economic importance. The fruit is made up of a smooth outer layer, a fibrous

*Figure 9–2* Coconut. Left to right: Fruit as it comes from tree. With outer rind removed to show coir. Coir removed, exposing shell; this is the way coconuts usually appear in markets in the United States. Shell broken to expose the meat. Coconut water.

middle layer, or coir, and a strong inner portion, or shell, that encloses the single seed. Frequently coconuts appearing in markets in the United States have had the outer layers of the fruit removed so that the shell is exposed. The seed, in addition to the embryo, has a thin, papery outer layer; inside this layer are the "meat," or kernel, and the "coconut water," which together form the endosperm, or reserve food for the embryo. The coconut seed is one of the largest known.*

Coconuts, like bananas, need plenty of warmth and moisture and good drainage. They are mostly found near the coast but do grow considerably inland in some regions. Florida is the farthest away from the equator they are known to grow. Although many are now grown on plantations, they are still a crop on small holdings in many places. Ninety percent of all coconuts are grown in southeastern Asia. The Philippines is now the largest producer, and coconuts rank as the number one cash crop in that country. Indonesia, which until World War II held the first position, is now second in production, followed by India and Sri Lanka. Mexico is the chief producer outside of southeastern Asia.

---

*The distinction of having the largest seed apparently belongs to another palm, *Lodoicea maldivica*, known as the double coconut, Seychelles nut, or *coco de mer*, which has a fruit two or three times the size of the coconut and weighing up to forty pounds. Marvelous tales were once told of the fruits that washed up on the shores of India from their homeland in the Seychelles Islands.

Coconut trees have been reported to bear 500 nuts a year, but 50 to 100 seems to be a more normal production. Harvesting is usually done by climbing the trees or by cutting the nuts with knives attached to long bamboo poles; more rarely the nuts are allowed to fall to the ground and are then collected. Monkeys reportedly have been trained to harvest coconuts in Sarawak, Indonesia, and Thailand. The name *Cocos* itself relates to monkeys but has nothing to do with their harvesting the fruit. The word, which comes from the Portuguese, means monkey's face, a reference to the three eyes in the shell that make it resemble the face of a monkey.

After the nuts are harvested they are cut in half, and the meat is gouged out immediately or after partial drying in the sun. The meat is then cured, by sun drying where weather permits or in kilns, to produce copra. The moisture content must be drastically reduced or the copra deteriorates rapidly. After the drying, the oil, which forms 60 to 70 percent of the copra, is extracted. Primitive methods using stone or wooden mortars and pestles, powered by humans or bullocks, are still employed in parts of India, but these have been replaced by hydraulic presses in most other coconut-producing areas. The oil is the most important commercial product derived from the coconut. Its greatest use in the last century was in the manufacture of soaps. All floating soaps were made from coconut oil until fairly recently, when it was found that soaps made from other oils would float if air was pumped through them during manufacture. Coconut oil is still regarded as one of the best for making soaps, and considerable amounts are still used for that purpose. In this century, however, its chief use has been for margarine, and it was the main oil used for that purpose until recently, but soybean and cottonseed oils have come largely to replace it. Since coconut oil is composed of 90 percent saturated fatty acids, it is not as highly recommended for human food as many of the other vegetable oils, which are largely unsaturated.

The residue, or coconut cake, left after oil extraction is used chiefly to feed livestock. The coconut cake is a rich source of both protein— one of the most nearly complete proteins of all vegetable sources—and carbohydrates. Although it is more fibrous than most other oil-seed residues and hence difficult to digest, it is nevertheless unfortunate that more of it is not processed for human food, for coconuts are mostly grown in areas where protein deficiency is common.

The meat of either immature or mature coconuts is used directly for human food in many areas where these palms are grown. Although it is the chief vegetable protein source for some people, it is usually served

*Figure 9–3* *A*. Coconut tree in fruit. (Courtesy of FAO.) *B*. Monkey harvesting coconut. (Courtesy of Sa-korn Trinandwan.) *C*. Coconut "monkey face."

mixed with other foods as a vegetable, and nowhere does it appear to be a basic food staple as do most of the plants we have discussed. The per capita consumption is estimated to be 140 nuts a year in Sri Lanka and is probably considerably greater than this among Polynesians in some of the Pacific Islands. In many countries of the temperate zones, dried coconut is used mostly for candies and cakes. Desiccated coconut meat was first made in England and the United States in the last part of the past century and is a fairly important use of coconut meat today.

The fibrous part of the fruit, the husk, or coir, also has a number of uses. It makes a fine rope, resistant to sea water, and its use for this purpose is quite ancient. Coir is also used to make mats, rugs, and filters, and stuffing for furniture. India is the world's greatest producer. To prepare the fibers, the husks are immersed in saline backwaters for several months for retting, and the fibers are then separated by beating the husks with wooden mallets or clubs.

The young inflorescence, or flower cluster, of the coconut, like that of several other palms, yields a sweet juice, or toddy, when tapped. The toddy, which is mostly sucrose, is sometimes drunk fresh; more frequently it is used to prepare alcoholic beverages, such as arrack, or vinegar. In Sri Lanka more than eight million gallons of arrack are produced annually, very little of it being exported. Small amounts of toddy are also used for making sugar.

The shells have a number of uses, the most ancient of which are as eating or drinking utensils and for fuel. They are still used for these purposes as well as for bowls for hookah pipes and for the manufacture of novelties or "artistic objects"; when ground they are used as a filler in plastics. The coconut water makes a refreshing drink, and in recent years has been used by plant physiologists as a growth-promoting substance. The large leaves, which reach lengths of twelve feet, are used for thatching and for making baskets and hats.* The wood is used to some extent in construction and furniture making, and forms some of the "porcupine wood" of commerce. The palm heart, or "cabbage," the tender bud at the apex of the stem, is sometimes eaten, but not as frequently as that of some other palms, for once the bud is removed the tree dies. The coconut is also still used as a religious offering in some parts of southeastern Asia, probably stemming from the ancient belief that the coconut is the "Tree of Heaven"—*Kalpa Vrikska* in India—

---

*They are apparently second only to the leaves of the Panama hat palm for this purpose. The Panama hat palm isn't a true palm but, rather, belongs to the family Cyclanthaceae.

*Figure 9–4*   Extracting coconut meat for copra, Caroline Islands. (Courtesy of S. F. Glassman.)

or the "Tree of Life." There is also a belief among certain people of New Guinea that the first coconut tree sprang from the head of the first man to die.

Two main groups of coconut palms are recognized—dwarf forms and tall forms. Numerous varieties exist within each group, differing primarily in the shape, size, coloring, and yield of the fruit. Although seed selection for high yield probably is fairly ancient, there has been very little modern scientific breeding work on the coconut. There are several reasons for this. First of all, it is a tropical crop, and as we have already seen for other plants, these have received much less attention than the crops of the temperate zone, where more plant breeders and money for research are available. Moreover, the coconut is often a small landholder's crop rather than a plantation crop, and governments seldom do as much for small farmers as they do for the big ones. Nor can small landholders employ breeders, as do some of the companies that have extensive holdings. Another factor responsible for the limited improvement of the coconut is that breeding work with a tree always takes longer than that with annual or herbaceous perennial plants. It takes three years for a dwarf coconut palm to bear fruit and five to seven years for the tall varieties. From time of flowering to fruit maturity is nearly a year. Germination of the seed requires about four months, time enough for a full growth cycle in some annual crops. Thus, the breeding of superior varieties of the coconut through hybridization requires many years of work.

The place of origin of the coconut has been the subject of some controversy in the past. There were some who held that it was a native of the New World, primarily because all of its close relatives are American. Others maintained that the coconut was native to the Indo-Pacific region, pointing out that it was a much more extensively used plant in that area than in the Americas. While it is true that the coconut does have most of its close relatives among the American palms, there is now general agreement among botanists that it originated in the Indo-Pacific region. Among some of the most convincing evidence that has been brought forward since the original controversy is the discovery of fossil *Cocos* of late Tertiary age in New Zealand and India, proving that a species of coconut did inhabit the Pacific region before modern man appeared on the scene. The coconut was present in both Asia and the Americas previous to 1492. At that time, however, it was known only from western Panama in the Americas, and its wide distribution in the New World came about in historical times. Its presence in Panama previous to the arrival of the Spanish can probably be explained without invoking human aid, for coconuts are able to float in sea water for more than 100 days, which would allow ample time for a fruit to float across the Pacific. Probably the establishment of coconuts in new areas through the agency of ocean currents is a rare event, but it would need to have happened only once to explain the plant's presence in the New World. People, as well as ocean currents, are probably responsible for its wide distribution on the Pacific Islands. How early the coconut first became a domesticated plant is not known. It was grown in India by 1000 BC but it may not have been first domesticated there.

Two tales concerning coconuts have been widely circulated. One is the story of the coconut crab, or robber crab. According to the account given by Darwin, this crab tears the husk from the coconut "fibre by fibre," exposing the three eyes on the shell, and then hammers on one of the eyes with its heavy claw until a hole is made, after which it extracts the coconut meat with its pincers. Apparently Darwin's leg was being pulled by a Mr. Leish, whom he credits as his source, for Child points out that no one has ever seen a crab in nature perform this remarkable feat, and in feeding experiments the crabs have died when coconuts were the only food offered them. The second story, concerning the finding of pearls inside coconuts, also has never been substantiated, according to Child. The so-called coconut pearls in museums have been shown to come from molluscs. There is, however, a recent account* in which it is claimed that there is scientific evidence that on very rare occasions "pearls" do develop in coconuts.

---

*J. Baltes, Ueber die Kokosperle. *Fette Seifen Anstrichmittel* 73: 1–4, 1971.

# 10

# *More oils:*
# *sunflower and cotton*

*Everything is soothed by oil*
Pliny the Elder. *Natural History, Book II*

*Cotton is King*
David Christy, 1855

Fats and oils not only provide a more concentrated source of energy than do carbohydrates and proteins but also are a necessary part of the human diet. In recent years there has been a great increase in the demand for oils of vegetable origin, particularly for making shortening and margarine; the latter has largely replaced butter in many parts of the world. The reasons are twofold: vegetable oils are usually cheaper than animal oils; and animal fats and oils contain saturated fatty acids that may be harmful to our health, whereas many plants contain polyunsaturated fatty acids that may be beneficial. A number of plants furnish edible oils. As was pointed out in an earlier chapter, the soybean is the world's chief source. Other plants contributing large amounts are sunflowers, peanuts, palms—chiefly the coconut and the African oil palm—rape (see p. 194), and cotton. Corn oil is of considerable importance in the United States for cooking and for making margarine. In addition to their use for food, many plant oils also have considerable use in industry.

*Figure 10–1* Field of cultivated sunflowers in North Dakota. (Courtesy of Arelém Advertising, Inc.)

The jojoba *(Simmondsia chinensis)*, a wild shrub of the arid southwestern United States and northern Mexico, has been found to possess an "oil" in its seed that is actually a liquid wax. The possible industrial applications include the making of lubricants that can withstand extremely high temperatures and pressures. Presently lubricants of this type are obtained from the sperm oil of whales. The potential significance of jojoba oil becomes clear when it is realized that whales are now endangered species. Attempts are now being made to bring the jojoba plant into cultivation.

## Sunflower

The sunflower *(Helianthus annuus)* is the only important crop plant to have been domesticated in what is now the United States. The wild sunflower was an important food source to seed gatherers in western North America, and people apparently carried it as a weed to the central United States, where it became domesticated sometime before 1000 BC. The Indians esteemed the sunflower seeds as food, as well as a source of oil; they also found many other uses for the plant. When the Europeans arrived they found the sunflower fairly widely cultivated in eastern North America as well as in the Southwest and in northern Mexico, although it was nowhere a major food plant. After its introduction into Europe in the sixteenth century, the sunflower was at first

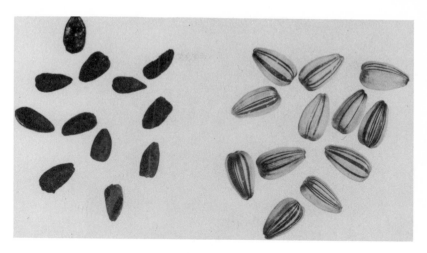

*Figure 10–2*  Achenes of sunflower from archaeological site in Ohio (left) and from modern variety. The archaeological achenes are charred and are probably 10 percent smaller than they were originally. (From *The Sunflower*, by Charles B. Heiser, Jr. Copyright © 1976 by the University of Oklahoma Press.)

*Figure 10–3*  The sunflower increased greatly in size with domestication. Wild sunflower (lower left); weed sunflower (upper left); and domesticated sunflower. (From *The Sunflower*, by Charles B. Heiser, Jr. Copyright © 1976 by the University of Oklahoma Press.)

*Figure 10–4*  Mammoth Russian sunflower; ornamental varieties may be seen in background. (From *The Sunflower*, by Charles B. Heiser, Jr. Copyright © 1976 by the University of Oklahoma Press.)

regarded as a curiosity, chiefly for the great size the plant could attain in a single season; it did not become a major food plant until it reached Russia. Large areas in Russia were found suitable for growing sunflowers, which soon became the Russians' major source of food oil. Today the Soviet Union leads the world in sunflower production. Much of the modern improvement of the sunflower was done in Russia, including an increase in oil content from 28 percent to around 50 percent and the development of semidwarf varieties that could be harvested mechanically. The sunflower also early became an important crop in the Balkans, a little later in Argentina, and more recently in several other countries. Although rather widely grown on a minor scale in the United States for many years, chiefly for bird seed, it has become important as an oil plant in this country only within the last ten years. A significant factor in the recent success of the sunflower as a major oil source was the development of high-yielding hybrids using a cytoplasmic male-sterile line. Although the sunflower is cultivated today

*Figure 10–5*   Cotton plant in fruit. (Courtesy of the USDA.)

chiefly for its fine oil, fair amounts are still grown to supply seeds for confections such as "sunflower nuts," and for feeding birds. The seed cake left after the removal of the oil is a protein-rich food used for feeding livestock.

The cultivated sunflower is an annual plant that produces a single stalk bearing a massive head with numerous small flowers. Each flower has an ovary that produces a dry fruit known as an achene, which contains a single seed. Wild sunflowers, in contrast, are much branched plants that bear numerous heads; they also produce much smaller achenes. The American Indians had produced a domesticated plant little inferior to modern varieties, except for the yield of oil, long before the arrival of the Europeans.

The sunflower is a member of the plant family Compositae, which is the second largest family of the flowering plants. Only the orchid family is larger. In spite of its size the family has furnished few other food plants, lettuce *(Lactuca sativa)* perhaps being the most important.

The Jerusalem artichoke, or "sunchoke" *(Helianthus tuberosus)*, grown for its edible tuber, is a perennial sunflower and, like the sunflower itself, was domesticated in temperate North America. The safflower *(Carthamus tinctorius)*, of Old World origin, is another member of this family. Apparently originally domesticated for its flowers, which were used for a dye, it was subsequently grown for the oil content of its seeds. Because of its high content of polyunsaturated fatty acids, safflower oil is considered one of the finest for human consumption. Although the family Compositae has supplied few food plants, it more than makes up for this with a large number of very showy ornamentals, including marigolds, zinnias, chrysanthemums, and various forms of the sunflower.

## Cotton

Although cotton is a very old domesticated plant, its use as an oil crop is only a little over a century old. Still the world's most important vegetable fiber, producing more fiber for clothing than all other textiles combined, it now also ranks as one of the major sources of vegetable oil and stock feed, both derived from its seed. The fiber, called lint, comes from hairs on the seed. Before the seeds were used for oil those not needed for planting were discarded. For every 500 pound bale of cotton, 900 pounds of seeds are available for oil, seed meal and other uses.

The several species of cotton were originally shrubby or sometimes treelike perennials, but under domestication annuals developed. The rather large flowers produce a capsular fruit known as a boll. Cotton is a member of the Malvaceae, or mallow family, which is better known for its ornamentals, such as hollyhock and *Hibiscus*, than for food plants. Okra, or gumbo *(Abelmoschus esculentus)*, of Old World origin, is one of the few species now fairly widely grown as a vegetable.

Four different species of cotton have been brought into cultivation. *Gossypium herbaceum* was domesticated in Africa, and *Gossypium arboreum*, probably derived from it, was grown in India. Cloth fragments from India dated at around 3000 BC indicate considerable antiquity for the Old World cottons. In the New World, two species were also brought under domestication, *Gossypium hirsutum* in Mexico and *Gossypium barbadense* in western South America. There is archaeological evidence for the existence of *Gossypium hirsutum* around 2500 BC and for *Gossypium barbadense* about a thousand years later. A study of the chromosomes

*Figure 10–6* Harvesting cotton in Arizona. A mechanical harvester can pick as much in an hour as a man could pick in 72 hours. (Courtesy of the USDA.)

of these species revealed that the Old World cottons were diploid and the New World cottons tetraploid. It was further found that the New World cottons had one chromosome set, designated AA, identical to that of the Old World cottons, and a second set, designated DD, that was different. Thus it was apparent that the New World cottons owed their origin to hybridization between species with the AA and DD sets followed by chromosome doubling. Wild diploid species of *Gossypium* exist in the Americas with the DD set, but no species with the AA set occur there. When this was learned, some people postulated that humans must have been responsible for carrying an AA species from the Old World to the New to allow for the hybridization to take place. More recently, however, this hypothesis has been largely replaced by one that

*Figure 10–7*   Cotton. Leaf (right); boll at maturity (upper left); seed with lint and with lint removed (lower left).

has the Old World species arriving in the Americas by natural means, perhaps by seed drifting across the Atlantic. It is now thought that the New World tetraploid cottons developed before humans appeared on the scene, or when humankind was still in its infancy.

The American cottons are superior to those of the Old World and gradually largely replaced them. *Gossypium hirsutum*, earlier maturing than *Gossypium barbadense* and hence more resistant to boll weevil, is said to furnish 95 percent of the cotton grown in the world today. The United States and the Soviet Union are the world's leading producers. The southwestern United States, where the crop is grown under irrigation, has replaced the southeastern states, where cotton was once King, as the chief area of production in the United States.

The boll weevil, a beetle commemorated in song, entered the United States from Mexico late in the last century and has proved to be the most serious pest of cotton. Losses to the crop have been estimated at over \$200,000,000 a year. Breeding work devoted to securing resistant types and varieties that mature before the beetle has completed its life cycle has proven valuable, but the boll weevil continues to be a problem in some places. Large amounts of chemical herbicides, insecticides, and defoliants (used to remove the leaves to make harvesting easier) are used on the cotton crop and have raised concern over the resulting environmental pollution.

Cottonseed oil is used mostly for the production of shortening and margarine. The seed meal that remains after the extraction of the oil is a protein-rich food, at present used mostly for animal feed but potentially of greater use for humans. In 1949 the Institute of Nutrition of Central America and Panama (INCAP) was formed, and one of its most significant achievements to date has been the development of a vegetable flour, incaparina (from INCAP and harina, the Spanish word for flour), made largely from cottonseed meal. Incaparina is 25 percent or more protein. Its creation was an attempt to improve the diet of Latin Americans, who subsist mostly on maize and hence often suffer from protein deficiency. Incaparina sells at about one-fourth the cost of milk and has about the same nutritional value. In Central America and Panama about two million pounds per year were sold in the late sixties, but apparently much of this went to the middle classes. Some of the poor who most need it do not use it, either because they do not like its taste or because they are too poor to buy it.

A problem in the use of cotton products for food is that the plants have glands that produce a toxic substance, gossopol, which must be removed before its products can be eaten by non-ruminant animals. Gossopol is now removed chemically, but the process is expensive and reduces the value of the protein. Plant breeders have succeeded in producing glandless plants, but these are more susceptible to insect damage than the plants with glands. It should be noted that in 1979 the Chinese announced the development of a male contraceptive, called gossopol, from the cotton seed.

# 11

# Other plants for food, beverage, and spice

*Cauliflower is nothing but cabbage with a college education.*
Mark Twain, *Pudd'nhead Wilson's Calendar*

Although we can, and sometimes do, live solely on the basic foods, we usually use other plants as food or beverage with every meal. Some of these other foods are eaten primarily to add variety to the diet and to increase the enjoyment of eating, but at the same time many of them are excellent sources of vitamins and minerals and also supply small amounts of carbohydrates, proteins, and fats. Primitive people, as pointed out in the first chapter, almost certainly exploited a great array of wild food plants, and they continued to use some wild plants as fruits and vegetables after the domestication of the cereals. Eventually some of these fruits and vegetables were cultivated, and in time they became completely domesticated species. People today still utilize wild food sources in many parts of the world, often out of necessity but sometimes by preference. The collecting of wild foods has become an interesting hobby for many people in the United States.*

---

*Many of the "wild" foods being gathered in the United States are introduced species that have escaped from cultivation rather than native wild plants. Wild asparagus, wild carrots (also known as Queen Anne's lace), prickly lettuce, chicory, and burdock, for example, are plants that were introduced, either intentionally or accidentally, from the Old World and have become widespread weeds in North America. The Jerusalem artichoke and cattail, also used as wild food sources, are native North American species.

Vegetables

*Vegetable* has no precise botanical meaning in reference to food plants, and we find that almost all parts of plants have been employed as vegetables—roots (carrot and beet), stems (Irish potato and asparagus), leaves (spinach and lettuce), leaf stalk (celery and Swiss chard), bracts (globe artichoke), flower stalks and buds (broccoli and cauliflower), fruits (tomato and squash), seeds (beans), and even the petals (Yucca and pumpkin). A great many different plant families have provided our vegetables, but just as certain families have been particularly important in giving us our staples, so too have certain others in giving us vegetables.

The mustard family, or Cruciferae, has been particularly significant for its vegetables, and a single species, *Brassica oleracea*, has provided us with the cole crops, which include cabbage, kale, Brussels sprouts, cauliflower, broccoli, and kohlrabi. The kohlrabi, although often cultivated in in the United States, is seldom seen in markets. In this variety the stem enlarges above ground level to produce an edible tuber. The ancestor of all the cole crops was native to the Mediterranean region, and some think that it was first used for its oily seeds. Selection with emphasis on different parts of the plant eventually produced the diversity of cultivated varieties we now enjoy.

Other species of *Brassica*, originally native to either Europe or Asia, account for a number of other vegetables. These include plants grown for their roots—the turnip and rutabaga—and a great number whose leaves are eaten, collectively designated as the mustards. Two of these, brown mustard and black mustard, have seeds that are widely used in the preparation of the condiment, mustard, which, after black pepper, is the most widely used spice in the United States. Mustard is also used in medicine as a rubefacient, or counterirritant. Recently oil from the seed of the rape plants (*Brassica campestris* and *Brassica napus*) has become one of the world's major vegetable oils. Rape has been grown mostly in India and China, but it has become a major crop in Canada in recent years. The radish (*Raphanus sativus*) is another Old World member of the mustard family employed for food. Although radishes are ordinarily used only as a salad ingredient or relish in many places, they have an important role as a food plant in the Orient. Japanese varieties may reach weights of 65 pounds. They are used as a cooked vegetable, often stored for use in the winter, and are also fed to livestock. In parts of Asia, one variety of radish is especially grown for its seed pods, which may reach lengths of two feet and are used as a vegetable.

*Wild type*

*Kale*

*Cabbage*

*Cauliflower*

*Brussels sprouts*

*Broccoli*

*Kohlrabi*

*Figure 11–1* Variation in *Brassica oleracea*. By selection man has produced varieties valued for their leaves (kale and cabbage), specialized buds (Brussels sprouts), flowering shoots (cauliflower and broccoli), and enlarged stems (kohlrabi).

Of equal or greater importance for its contributions to our vegetables, is the cucurbit family (Cucurbitaceae). Five different species of squash or kin, belonging to the genus *Cucurbita*, were domesticated in the Americas. Some of these rank among the oldest known foods of the Americas, being recorded in archaeological deposits from 7000 BC in Mexico. Since the wild cucurbits have little or no flesh in the fruit, it has been postulated that they may have been domesticated for their edible seeds—"pepitas", or pumpkin seeds, are still eaten. Mutant types with fleshy fruits then appeared, according to the theory, and their deliberate selection has produced the thick-fleshed varieties now widely cultivated. The squashes and pumpkins, along with maize and beans, were carried north from Mexico and became important food plants of the North American agricultural Indians. Following the European discovery of America, pumpkins and squashes were soon introduced into Europe and Asia, and today they are important in many parts of the world not only for human food but for livestock as well. The Old World has also furnished food plants from the Cucurbitaceae, including the cucumber, the melons such as cantaloupe and cassaba, and the watermelon. The cucumber and the melons come from different species of the genus *Cucumis;* the watermelon belongs to the genus *Citrullus.*

The bottle gourd (*Lagenaria siceraria*), another member of the Cucurbitaceae, has never been more than a minor food plant, but has been valued for its hard-shelled fruits, which have been used as containers, for musical instruments, and for floats, as well as in other ways. This species is thought to be native to Africa, but archaeological remains of the fruit have been found in both Peru and Mexico dated at 7000 BC or earlier, and from the historical record we know that it is a very old cultivated plant of both India and China. Some have thought that people may have been responsible for its wide dispersal in early times, but since it has been shown that the gourds can remain in sea water for long periods without damage to the seeds, it is perhaps more likely that its wide distribution is to be explained as the result of oceanic drifting of the fruits. It was probably the most widely distributed domesticated species in prehistoric times and continues to be fairly widely used throughout much of the tropics.

The nightshade family, or Solanaceae, in addition to providing the Irish potato has supplied us with several other food plants, including the tomato (*Lycopersicon esculentum*), which has become one of the world's most important vegetables. The tomato was already a well established cultivated plant in Mexico when the Spanish arrived. It reached Europe in the first half of the sixteenth century and somehow acquired the

*Figure 11–2*  A harvest of bottle gourds, showing variation in the fruits. (From *The Gourd Book*, by Charles B. Heiser, Jr. © 1979 by the University of Oklahoma Press.)

reputation of being harmful to eat, for reasons that are not entirely clear. It seems likely that it was recognized as a member of the night-shade family, known to Europeans of the time as comprising only poisonous plants such as deadly nightshade, henbane, and mandrake, and that people were therefore reluctant to eat it.

Although the tomato is regarded as a vegetable, the part that is eaten is, botanically speaking, the fruit. Tomatoes are known with yellow, orange, pink, and green fruits in addition to the familiar red types. One of the first tomatoes to reach Italy was a yellow-fruited variety called *pomi d'oro* (apple of gold), which somehow became transformed to *poma amoris* (apple of love). The name love apple soon became attached to the tomato, not because of any real or supposed aphrodisiac property but simply through translation of the transformed Italian name. Only in this century did the tomato finally become widely appreciated for the fine food that it is. Remarkable changes have been achieved by plant breeders in recent years, one of which is the development of tomatoes with special characteristics that allow them to be mechanically har-vested. However, some of the varieties developed for long-distance win-

*Figure 11–3* Tomatoes that are tough skinned, even-ripening, readily detachable, and of a uniform size have been developed for machine harvesting. A mechanical harvester is in the background. (Courtesy of USDA.)

ter shipping to northern markets are inferior in taste to those grown in the home garden.

Among other plants in the Solanaceae grown for their fruits are the eggplant and the sweet and hot, or red, peppers. The eggplant, a species of *Solanum*, apparently had its origin in India and, like the tomato, was regarded with suspicion when it first reached Europe. One name for it at that time was mad apple, for it was thought that the eating of eggplant would produce insanity. Several different peppers, species of *Capsicum*, were domesticated in tropical America for their pungent fruits and became almost indispensable in the diet of many Indians. In post-Columbian times peppers became widely dispersed, and they have become as important in parts of southeastern Asia and Africa as they are in their homeland. Sweet peppers, a variety of *Capsicum annuum* (Figure 12-1), which also includes cayenne and chili peppers, have become more important in the temperate zones than have the pungent forms.

The parsley family (Umbelliferae) has provided several important vegetables, as well as many of our spices. In addition to parsley (*Petroselinum crispum*), whose leaves are used in cooking and for garnishing and whose roots are sometimes eaten, the roots of the carrot (*Daucus carota*), the parsnip (*Pastinaca sativa*), and the leaf stalk of celery (*Apium graveolens*), all plants of Old World origin, are widely used vegetables. Celeriac is a variety of celery grown for its large edible root. The arracacha (*Arracacia xanthorrhiza*), or zanahoria blanca ("white carrot"), is another excellent vegetable whose use is little known outside of its homeland in the Andes. To this family also belongs the deadly plant called poison hemlock, native to the Old World but widely naturalized in the United States.

## Fruits

Fruits, wild or cultivated, must have always been a source of pleasure because of their sweetness. Like vegetables, they come from many different families of plants, but in the north temperate zone one family—the rose family, or Rosaceae—stands out. Among its more important contributions are the apple and the pear, or pome fruits, species native to West Europe and Asia; various species of stone fruits, genus *Prunus*, including the peach, cherry, plum, and apricot, most of which also come from the Old World (although species of cherry and plum were also domesticated in the Americas); and the "berry"* fruits, black-berry, raspberry, and strawberry, with domesticated species from both the New and the Old World. Although these are rightly called temperate-zone fruits, some of them are cultivated at high altitudes near the equator.

Tropical and subtropical fruits abound, but only a small number, such as bananas, pineapple, figs, and the citrus fruits reach the temperate-zone markets with any regularity. The citrus fruits, whose nutritional value is widely recognized, are all members of the family Rutaceae, and a single genus, *Citrus*, supplies us with the most important species—sweet, bitter or sour, and mandarin orange (one form of the last known as the tangerine in the United States), lemon, lime, grapefruit, citron, and shaddock, or pumelo. All of these originated in southeastern Asia, with the exception of the grapefruit, which is thought to have been derived from the shaddock after the latter was introduced in the West Indies. The citrus plant is a small tree, often somewhat spiny, and has attractive, fragrant flowers. The fruit is a special type of berry known as a hesperidium. Its thick, leathery rind bears numerous oil glands that yield an essential oil widely used in flavoring.

Scientific proof of the importance of the citrus fruits came in 1756, when John Lind, a surgeon in the English navy, found that the scurvy common among seamen at the time could be prevented by eating oranges and lemons. Later in the century the Royal Navy began to provide rations of lime or lemon juice to its men, and the name "limey" came into use for British sailors as a result. Not until 1933 was vitamin C (ascorbic acid) identified as the factor responsible for the prevention of scurvy.

## Nuts

Nuts of various kinds have long served as a highly concentrated source of nutrition. From the archaeological record we know that nuts of

---

*Most of the so-called berry fruits do not have fruits that are classified as berries according to the botanical definition. A true berry is defined as a fleshy, many-seeded, indehiscent fruit that develops from the ovary of a single flower. Examples are grape, tomato, pumpkin, and orange. The raspberry and blackberry are in reality aggregate fruits in that they develop from many ovaries of a single flower. The individual fruitlets, or seed-bearing structures, of a blackberry, for example, are each the product of a single ovary and each is the equivalent of a plum in that it has a single seed enclosed in a fleshy covering. The strawberry is defined as an accessory fruit, for the fleshy part develops from a structure other than the ovary. The true fruits of a strawberry are the small, hard, straw-colored "seeds" on the surface.

various wild plants were a frequent source of food in prehistoric times. The word nut, as popularly used, is applied to the fruit or seed of a great number of plants, mostly trees. Botanically, a nut is defined as a hard and indehiscent one-seeded fruit; of the "nuts" utilized by various peoples, only a few, such as the acorn, the chestnut, and the hazelnut, meet the botanical definition. Acorns from various species of oaks, in both the Old and the New World, were at one time an important source of food. Many of the Indian tribes of the west coast of North America relied on acorns as their principal food source, and they devised various ways of leaching the tannins and bitter principles from them in order to make them palatable. Acorns are still sometimes used as a food source by the poorer people in some of the Mediterranean countries of Europe. The Eurasian chestnut continues to be a food plant in southern Europe, but the native American chestnut, whose nuts were once widely sought, has been practically eliminated by a blight disease that swept through the eastern United States at the beginning of this century. Acorns and chestnuts are valued as foods because of their high carbohydrate content.

Among the nuts with a particularly high protein content are the almond and the pistachio, both old cultivated plants of the Mediterranean region. The almond belongs to the same genus as the stone fruits, but the fleshy covering is poorly developed and the seed is the only part eaten. The almonds produced in the United States are grown in California.

Nuts with a high oil content include the Brazil nut and the cashew, both native to Brazil, the pecan of the central and southern United States, walnuts, and hazelnuts. The walnut foremost in use for food comes from the English, or Persian, walnut tree, which originally came from Iran. California is today one of the leading areas for walnut production. The native American black walnut is more valued for its wood than for its nuts. The hazelnut, or filbert, of Europe is also an important yielder of nuts. There are also native American species of hazelnuts.

## Beverages

It was early discovered that parts of certain plants had a pleasant stimulating effect,* and today many of these plants serve as the chief sources of nonalcoholic beverages. The four most significant of these are coffee,

---

*Exactly how the effects of certain of these plants were discovered is somewhat of a puzzle, for some of them have little or no stimulating action unless they are specially cured or processed.

*Figure 11–4*   Coffee berries. (Courtesy of FAO.)

tea, cacao, or chocolate, and maté, or Paraguay tea. These plants, all members of different botanical families, share one important feature in common: the possession of caffeine or a very similar alkaloid that is responsible for their stimulating property. Except for cacao, these plants offer little or nothing in the way of nutrition, and hence are hardly essential. Even though coffee and tea are not, strictly speaking, food plants, they are extremely important export crops in many parts of the tropical world and figure prominently in the economic welfare of many countries.

From a commercial standpoint coffee is the world's foremost beverage plant, although more people probably drink tea. Native to Ethiopia, coffee was carried to Arabia over 500 years ago, and for two centuries

Arabia was the principal producer. Coffee was later found to be well adapted to many parts of the American tropics, from elevations near sea level to 6000 feet, and today Brazil leads in the world's production. The United States is the world's chief importer of coffee, but per capita consumption is said to be greater in Sweden. The coffee plant (*Coffea arabica*) is a small tree or shrub with shiny, dark green leaves and numerous clusters of white flowers. Each of the berries contains two seeds called coffee beans. Following harvest, a process of fermentation and roasting is required before the beans assume their distinctive odor and flavor.

Tea (*Camellia sinensis*) also a small tree or shrub, is indigenous to India and China, where most of the world's production is concentrated today. The young leaves are carefully collected and then sorted to yield the various grades of tea. The post-harvesting processing is responsible for producing the different flavors of tea. Green teas are produced by drying and rolling the leaves, and black teas result from a fermentation during the drying process. It probably will come as no surprise that Great Britain is the world's greatest importer of tea.

Chocolate and cocoa come from the cacao plant (*Theobroma cacao*—theobroma, from the Greek, means "food of the Gods"), native to lowland tropical America and apparently first domesticated in Mexico. Details of its origin, like that of many of our domesticated plants, remain to be elucidated. When the Spanish reached Mexico, they found chocolate to be a prized drink among the Aztecs. Cacao beans, in fact, were once considered so valuable that they served as currency. The cacao plant is a small tree with rather large leaves and is unusual in that it bears its small flowers, and eventually its pods, close to the trunk and branches. The pod, a specialized berry, yields several rather large seeds or "beans." Following fermentation (a rather odorous process), drying, and roasting, the seeds are ready to be ground. The whole bean gives us chocolate, which is a rich food as well as a tasty drink, for it contains about 30 to 50 percent oil, 15 percent starch, and 15 percent protein. Cocoa is produced by removing most of the fatty oils, which then are used as cocoa butter. Western Africa has replaced tropical America, where diseases have always plagued the trees, as the world's principal region of cacao production and now provides 75 percent of the world's supply. *Cola nitida*, whose seeds are the source of cola, widely used in soft drinks, is native to tropical West Africa and belongs to the same family as cacao. Much of the cola supply used in the United States is from trees cultivated in Jamaica. Caffeine from other sources, including that removed in making decaffeinated coffee, is also used in some soft drinks.

*Figure 11–5*   Cacao tree with pods. (Courtesy of Jorge Soria.)

*Figure 11–6*   Opened cacao pod, exposing the individual seeds, or beans. (Courtesy of USDA.)

Maté, or Paraguay tea, although less widely known than the previously discussed beverage plants, can hardly be said to be a minor beverage, since it is drunk by more than 20 million people in South America and some is exported to Europe and North America. Maté comes from the leaves of *Ilex paraguariensis*, a relative of the holly tree, and is cultivated in Brazil, Paraguay, and Argentina. The processing of the leaves and the preparation of the drink are somewhat similar to the methods used for tea. Traditionally in South America maté is drunk from a gourd cup through a metal straw.

Alcoholic beverages have already been mentioned in various places in this book, and it should be quite obvious by now that many different plants can be employed to prepare them. Few, however, can rival the grape. Grapes are, of course, one of our widely used fruits; they can be used fresh or as raisins, but most grapes go into the production of wine, with smaller amounts used to make brandy and cognac. The grape native to the Near East or surrounding area, *Vitis vinifera*, although not one of our earliest domesticates, is of considerable antiquity as a cultivated plant. Presumably the origin of wine, which is simply fermented grape juice, was not very complicated: someone squeezed some grape juice and let it stand, and wild yeasts converted some of the sugar in the grape to alcohol. Its preparation through the years, however, has become more elaborate.

The Bible tells us that Noah planted a vineyard, and in fact, wine is mentioned no fewer than 165 times in the Bible. Wine had probably been around for some time before it reached the Greeks and Romans, who made considerable improvement in the "art" of wine making. The grape vine was carried to France in 600 BC, and after Christianity became established monasteries played a significant role in establishing some of the great vineyards there. France and Italy were to become the world's foremost wine countries. Today Italy produces more wine than France, but France is generally regarded as producing the world's best wines. Consumption in France, with an average of about 30 gallons per capita annually, is slightly higher than in Italy. In the latter half of the eighteenth century there were devastating losses of the vines throughout Europe from diseases, and not until it was found that stems of *Vitis vinifera* could be grafted to rootstocks of the American species was there a recovery. It was perhaps only fitting that resistance to the diseases should have come from the American rootstocks, for the diseases came to Europe with the introduction of American vines in the first place. This was also the time of Louis Pasteur's great discoveries, some of which contributed directly to an improvement of the wine industry.

A

B

*Figure 11–7*  *A*. California vineyard in winter. (Courtesy of Wine Institute.) *B*. Harvesting the grapes. (Courtesy of Wine Institute.)

Attempts were made to grow *Vitis vinifera* in eastern North America soon after it was settled, but both the humid climate and the cold winters were unfavorable, and it was to be some time before people turned to the American species and achieved success. In 1852 the Concord grape (named for the town in Massachusetts) came into being, either as a mutant of the native fox grape or as a hybrid with *Vitis vinifera*. It was an immediate success, and its cultivation spread halfway across the continent in two years. The Concord and other native American grapes and hybrids of these with *Vitis vinifera* are the source of the wines of the Great Lakes region today. The Old World species, however, was very successful in the Mediterranean climate of California, where it was introduced by the Spanish late in the eighteenth century, and today it is the basis of the California wines. Although wine consumption has doubled in the United States in the last three years, the per capita consumption is still only slightly over two gallons a year. New methods of preparing wine, including mechanical harvesting and aging in stainless steel tanks, were introduced in California and are now spreading to Europe. *Vitis vinifera* is also fairly widely grown for the production of wines in other parts of the world, including Argentina and Chile, where the climate is suitable.

## Spices

In their search for edible plants primitive people must have discovered many of those that now supply us with spices and condiments, and they probably learned to use these aromatic plants to make food more flavorful or to help cover up the taste and odor of food that had passed its prime. In time some of the spice plants became intentionally cultivated, and with the Romans the spices came into their own in the art of cooking. Through Marco Polo's accounts Europeans became aware of the wealth of the spices of the Far East, and it was partly an attempt to secure these spices that led to the great ocean voyages of discovery in the fifteenth and sixteenth centuries.

Though hardly essential to nutrition spices often made eating more enjoyable, and a large number of spice plants are found among our domesticated species. Reference has already been made to red pepper and mustard. The botanical families that have made the greatest number of contributions to our spices are the mint family, or Labiatae, and the parsley family, or Umbelliferae. The former has given us basil, marjoram, oregano, rosemary, sage, savory, and thyme, as well as spearmint

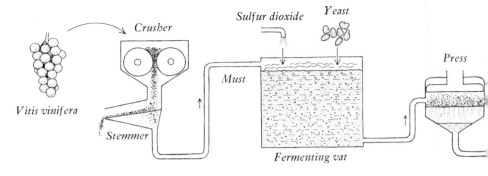

*Figure 11–8* The method of producing wine in California is similar to that of Europe. Shown here are the steps in the production of red wine. The grapes are crushed to produce a "must." The must goes to a fermenting vat where yeasts transform the sugar into alcohol and then to a press for the removal of the skin and seeds. The wine then moves to settling vats where a "fining" process removes impurities. After filtering and aging in casks, it is ready for bottling. (From "Wine" by Maynard A. Amerine. Copyright © 1964 by Scientific American, Inc. All rights reserved.)

and peppermint; the latter has contributed anise, caraway, celery, chervil, coriander, cumin, dill, fennel, and, of course, parsley. The vegetables contributed by the parsley family have already been mentioned; this family obviously must be considered one of major importance. The orchid family, which in number of species is the largest in the plant kingdom, has supplied only one plant that graces our food. Extract of vanilla comes from the pod of the vanilla orchid (*Vanilla planifolia*), native to tropical America. Although the plant is still cultivated for use as a flavoring, today most vanilla flavoring is made synthetically.

By far the world's most important spice is pepper (*Piper nigrum*), which at present accounts for one-fourth of the world's commerce in spices. The pepper plant is a member of the family Piperaceae and is not at all related to the *Capsicum* peppers previously mentioned. Apparently first domesticated in India, pepper became one of the first trade items between Europe and the Far East. Like many spices of the time, it was widely used in medicine as well as in seasoning and preserving food. The pepper plant is a woody vine, climbing to heights of 30 feet or more. The inconspicuous clusters of flowers each produce 50 to 60 fruits known as peppercorns. After drying, the whole peppercorns are ground to produce black pepper. If the hull is first removed, the ground product is white pepper. The plant is adapted to hot, wet,

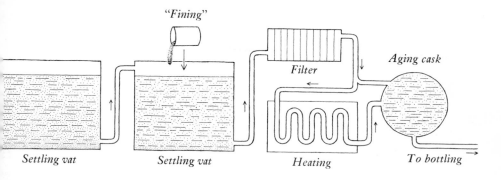

"Fining"

Filter

Aging cask

Settling vat           Settling vat           Heating           To bottling

tropical regions and today the bulk of the world's supply is produced in India and Indonesia. The United States is the chief importer.

Another spice, nutmeg, has received some notoriety as a hallucinogen in recent years. Its use for such purpose is actually quite ancient, and it was early recognized that overindulgence could be lethal. Nutmeg comes from a tree, *Myristica fragrans*, native to the Malay Archipelago and now cultivated in the West Indies as well as in its homeland. The pulverized seeds produce nutmeg, and a second spice, mace, is prepared from the outer growth of the seed.

There are, of course, many other plants used for food. A few of the well known and widely used, as well as many lesser known, have not been included in this survey. The present account should, however, give some indication of the great diversity of plants that serve in our diet.

# 12

# Evolution and breeding of the domesticates

*And he gave it for his opinion, that whoever could make two ears of corn, or two blades of grass, to grow upon a spot of ground where only one grew before, would deserve better of mankind, and do more essential service to his country, than the whole race of politicians put together.*

Jonathan Swift, *Gulliver's Travels*

*The practical plant-breeder uses this material [species, proles, varieties and forms] as bricks with which he must construct new forms. He now knows where to find definite construction material. The modern systematist, armed with physiology, cytology, genetics, and immunology, provides the practical plant-breeder with a new scientific foundation. The whole study of the initial material in plant-breeding is now quite different from what it was a few years ago. Modern differential systematics is elaborating a new chapter in plant-breeding, the knowledge of the initial material. On the basis of the differential study of the evolution and geography of species, it gives to the plant-breeder all his necessary constructional materials.*

N. I. Vavilov, *The New Systematics of Cultivated Plants*, 1940

With the domestication of plants and animals came changes in the domesticated organisms, at first largely unintentional. Today we are deliberately directing change in domesticated plants and animals in an effort to make them serve us more effectively. Modern evolutionary theory provides an understanding of how the changes occur.

The heredity of a plant or animal is controlled by its genes. Although genes are ordinarily very stable and copy themselves exactly generation after generation, spontaneous changes in them do occur. Such changes are known as gene mutations, and they may be passed on to the following generations. Through sexual reproduction genes are recombined in various ways, and thus it is possible for a species to "try out" various combinations of genes. Together mutation and recombination provide variation, the raw material of evolution. The force that acts upon this variation to produce change in a species is natural selection, which operates through differential reproduction. Thus, an organism with a particular combination of genes may produce more offspring than those with other combinations, or more of its offspring may survive and reproduce. In time such a successful combination will replace those that are less successful.

Once plants or animals are domesticated, the same evolutionary factors are at work: mutations and recombinations producing variability and selection serving to guide the changes. However, man instead of nature is the important selective agent. Thus in the process of domestication we find that artificial selection joined natural selection. The plants and animals, in turn, became dependent upon humans for their perpetuation and frequently lost the ability to survive under natural conditions. We have seen in previous chapters that many cereals and legumes have lost the mechanisms for seed dispersal and germination that allow them to compete in nature and have acquired characteristics, such as nondehiscent fruits and large seeds, that have made them better plants for our purposes.

Although the archaeological record has revealed a great deal about early human foods, it hasn't as yet told us how long the process of domestication took. Nor, perhaps, should it be expected to, for the process was such a gradual one that a sharp demarcation between wild species and early domesticated or semidomesticated species is difficult. Domesticated plants and animals usually differ in several ways from wild ones, and the differences are not acquired all at once. A species may, of course, continue to change after domestication is completed, as do many of our domesticates today. Domestication might be said to be completed when man controls the breeding of the organism, as was stated earlier.

The changes accompanying domestication could have occurred very rapidly in some organisms. The process probably did not require thou-

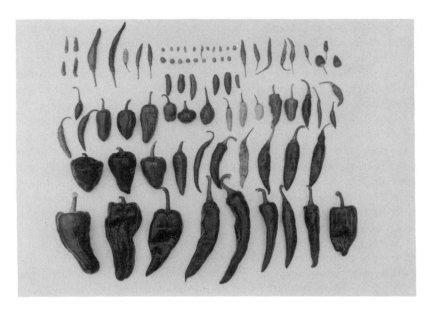

*Figure 12–1* Variation under domestication in the chili pepper *(Capsicum annuum)*. The wild plants have small, red, erect, deciduous, extremely pungent fruits (upper row, center). From these have been developed an array of forms, varying greatly in size, color, and pungency and including pendent and persistent fruits (shown with stalk) as well as erect and deciduous types.

sands of years, as implied by some writers on the subject. In fact, a few hundred years or less could have been enough time for some rather profound changes in a plant or animal under human influence. The time required would, of course, vary considerably from one organism to another and according to the type of selection that was exercised. Certainly annual plants, which produce a new generation every year, could have undergone a very rapid change.

The great Swiss botanist A. P. de Candolle pointed out a hundred years ago that no new basic food plants have been domesticated in historical times. This statement is still true and applies to animals as well as plants. How could primitive people have made such wise choices in their selection of plants and animals to domesticate? Although luck or chance may have played a role, I think that we must give the major credit to experimentation of a trial-and-error sort. People must have had an intimate acquaintance with all the food resources in their environment when they began the process of domestication. We don't know if they started their trials with the plants and animals that were difficult to obtain or with those that were common. It would seem reasonable that they started with those that they regarded as important—whether for religious reasons or because these were their favorite foods. Some of these experiments would have failed, and some of the early domesticates may have been replaced by others that were superior for one reason or another. The archaeological record wouldn't necessarily be expected to give testimony of the failures. Interesting evidence does exist, however, that certain North American Indians had a marsh elder (*Iva annua*), a relative of the ragweeds, that had fruits much larger than those of wild marsh elders today. It seems reasonable to suppose that these fruits, some of which are found stored in prehistoric sites, were used for food, but the plant apparently was replaced by superior foods before historical times.

Among the most important early domesticated plants were annuals with large or numerous seeds. Many of them were probably originally weeds that grew in open or disturbed habitats. In a sense they were preadapted to cultivation, since they were not only prolific but also could mature seeds in a space of a few months and were well suited to grow in man-made environments. It was therefore not entirely accidental that they gave rise to our most important food plants.

In an earlier chapter it was pointed out that certain animals—cattle, sheep, and goats, for example—were preadapted to human use since they could live on a diet that did not place them in competition with our ancestors. Moreover, the fact that they were gregarious rather than solitary animals would mean that they could be more readily kept and managed. As with plants, it is quite possible that attempts were made to domesticate other animals. We know that the ancient Egyptians did so.

The earliest type of selection in plants was probably not conscious. The loss of natural means of seed dispersal may serve as an example. When cereal was first brought into cultivation the plants had a brittle fruiting stalk that would shatter readily, allowing some of the grains to fall to the ground before they could be harvested. A mutant type that had a nonbrittle fruiting stalk might appear occasionally and would hold all its grain until harvested. Among seeds saved for planting there would likely be a high proportion from the plants with nonbrittle stalks. After the next year's sowing and harvest still more seeds from the mutant strain would be collected. This process, if repeated year after year, would lead to more and more of the plants with the nonbrittle stalks appearing in the next generations. For the nonbrittle type com-

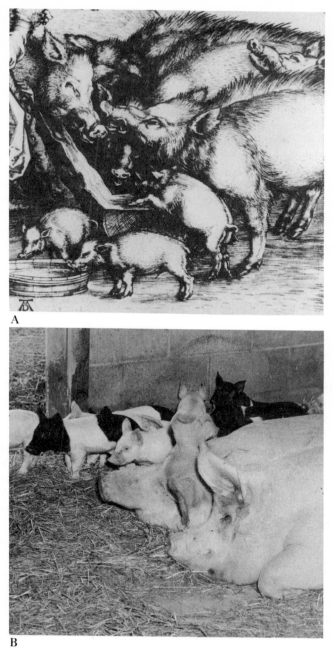

A

B

*Figure 12–2* *A*. Detail from Albrecht Dürer's *The Prodigal Son Amid The Swine* (1496). *B*. Present-day sows with young. Breeders have considerably changed the appearance and productivity of the pig. (Courtesy of USDA.)

pletely to replace the wild type considerable time would be required and would depend to a large degree upon the nature of the gene or genes controlling this particular character. If, however, people realized the advantage of the nonbrittle character and saved only seeds of this type for sowing, the character might become established fairly rapidly. In a like manner there would have been changes in animals. For example, when people captured animals, they would have found it difficult to take the most vicious and cunning. Or, if such animals were captured, they might have escaped or quickly ended up in the pot as their captors realized they couldn't be managed. Thus there would have been selection for the more docile animals to furnish stock for the next generation.

How early intentional selection was practiced is a matter of conjecture. As suggested in an earlier chapter, at first intentional selection may have been related to religious purposes. Whether or not this is so, artificial selection probably was not too long in coming after the domestication of plants and animals. For example, the realization must have been made quite early on that only one or a few males are necessary to perpetuate a flock or herd. We might suppose that only certain males were kept for service and that these may have been chosen for their color, the shape of their horns or the lack of horns, their docility, and so on. Later, of course, there would have been selection for milk, wool, or meat production and the other types of characters that we regard as the most important today. Such selection, of course, would lead to a gradual change in the animals. The length of time required for the establishment of a new character would depend upon the nature of its inheritance and the intensity with which breeding was managed.

Once people began to cultivate plants and keep animals, the evolution of these organisms was altered. The very act of growing plants and maintaining animals away from their natural habitats could have allowed the establishment of some variants that might have perished in nature. However, the new environment could not call forth desirable mutations; people still had to depend on chance mutation to produce variation in the first place.

When people began to move their plants and animals to some distance from their original habitat, they might have brought them into areas where other wild races or closely related species were located, permitting crossing to occur naturally. Such hybridization would have allowed new combinations of genes to appear. Some of the recombinants might have been desirable from the human standpoint. Thus there was a new source of variation that would have allowed for improvement of a domesticate and the creation of new varieties.

Another source of variability, and of the production of new varieties, would have been crossing between different strains of a domesticated species. If, as we may suppose, cattle were domesticated in different places, we might expect the different geographical strains to show some differences even though they originally came from the same wild species. Later, as people traveled with their herds or exchanged stock, opportunity would have existed for interbreeding.

Hybridization played an important role in the evolution of domesticated species, but isolation also played a very significant role. People at times would have taken their plants and animals into areas where the related wild types were not present. Thus, for example, in some places domesticated cattle would have been the only cattle, and they would thus have constituted a closed breeding population. Such a restriction on reproduction would favor the establishment of some of the variant types, since there would be no possibility of wild-type genes entering the domestic population. In fact, it seems likely that the most rapid evolution could have occurred by having periods of isolation followed by periods of hybridization. Some of the plants probably early provided their own method of isolation by becoming self-pollinating. Many of the cultivated plants, including many of the cereals, are habitually self-pollinating, although the wild types that gave rise to them were incapable of self-pollination.

Although early humans had no way of producing polyploid plants, it is possible that by bringing together two previously isolated species they created hybrids that spontaneously doubled their chromosome number to produce useful plants. Perhaps it was man, as previously pointed out, who brought the primitive wheats into contact with goat grasses, permitting the formation of the hybrids that gave rise to the bread wheats.

Selection continued to be the main, if not only, method of improving domesticated plants and animals for thousands of years. Spontaneous hybridization, as was pointed out above, doubtlessly contributed to important changes. Intentional hybridization of animals must be quite ancient, but hybridization as a deliberate method of improving plants is fairly recent. The first well-documented plant hybrids were made in the eighteenth century, and the aim was not to improve cultivated varieties but to prove that plants reproduced sexually. Gradually, intentional hybridization became used in an attempt to improve plants and with it "planning replaced accident" as C. D. Darlington has expressed it. However, until Mendel's laws were rediscovered in this century, the breeders were still working largely in the dark. Modern genetics gave plant and animal breeding a firm scientific base.

Today selection is still an important part of any breeding program, but it is accomplished in far more sophisticated ways than in past centuries. Hybridization both within and between species continues to serve as one of the principal tools of the breeder. Inbreeding followed by hybridization led to the greatly increased yields of maize. Hybridization in wheat and rice have been responsible for the development of the new "miracle" seeds that produced the Green Revolution. Many other plants and our principal domesticated animals have been greatly improved through hybridization.

With the artificial induction of mutations by X-rays in the late 1920s by H. J. Muller came the realization that the breeders had a potential new tool. Instead of having to depend upon nature to supply the variation, breeders could induce change by using X-rays and other mutagenic agents. Of course, most of the mutant types so produced are simply discarded, for most mutations—whether appearing at random in nature or as the result of a mutagenic agent—are deleterious, or at least not desirable. Efforts to use artificial mutations in plant breeding did persist, and now more than 90 commercially accepted varieties of cultivated plants exist that have resulted from induced mutations. Nature, however, continues to be the principal source of mutations used by the breeder and will continue to be so for some time to come.

The naturally occurring mutations include some very ancient ones found in older varieties of our domesticated plants and animals. Only recently has it been realized that there exists a tremendous reservoir of potentially valuable genes for use in breeding work in the old varieties of plants and animals. Although many of these varieties are rather unproductive it does not mean that they are worthless. As the new improved cereals and other modern varieties of plants and animals spread throughout the world, the older varieties are being lost at an alarming rate.* For this reason, seed banks for the preservation of plant germ plasm have now been established. A number of years ago the Rockefeller Foundation set up a corn bank to preserve as many of the Indian races of maize as possible, and various governments have taken

---

*There is some danger in any one variety being widely grown, for if it should prove susceptible to a new disease, the whole crop could be virtually wiped out at one time. The southern corn blight that appeared in the United States in 1970 is an example, for the disease attacked those hybrids that had a cytoplasmic male-sterile strain as a parent and did no damage to others. As most of the maize grown in the United States had such a parent, there was considerable loss. Thus there is an advantage to diversity, for it is unlikely that all varieties will prove equally susceptible to a disease.

*Figure 12–3* Rice breeder pollinating a flower to secure hybrid seed. (Courtesy of Rockefeller Foundation.)

similar steps to preserve the genetic resources of other plants. Much more needs to be done.

Various weedy species and wild species related to our domesticates still have much to contribute to breeding programs. It is up to the systematist to catalog this diversity and to indicate where it may be found. While this has been done for some groups of plants and animals, others have scarcely been touched. Botanical and zoological expeditions have been made to many parts of the earth to collect wild species and weeds, but some areas have yet to be intensively explored.

A large number of the major food plants—wheat, sugar cane, potatoes, sweet potatoes, and bananas among them—are polyploids. Just as scientists discovered how to induce mutation, they also found that polyploids could be created artificially. By treating plants with the chemical colchicine, and through other methods, they can induce chromosome doubling, which gives rise to polyploid plants. Great hopes were once held for the production of economically important plants by use of this method, for polyploids are often larger and more hardy than their diploid progenitors. The hopes have not been entirely realized, but some valuable ornamentals, forage plants, and fruits, the most interesting of which perhaps is the seedless watermelon, have been developed. The understanding of polyploidy, however, has allowed tremendous improvement in some of our polyploid crops. It has, for example, allowed the transfer of desirable genes from wild diploid species of goat grass (*Aegilops*) to the bread wheats by some most ingenious methods.

The traditional methods of breeding, chiefly through hybridization and selection, may have about reached their upper limits, particularly as far as improving the major crops such as wheat, rice, corn, and potatoes, so that new aims and approaches are called for. Among the aims would be such things as incorporating nitrogen fixation into the cereals and making photosynthesis itself more effective. At present only the legumes among the crop plants are able to fix nitrogen. If the cereals could somehow be induced to do so, it would drastically curtail the need for nitrogen fertilizer; at present fertilizers are so expensive that they are beyond the reach of many farmers of the world. Some have even suggested the possibility of hybridizing a grass and a legume in an attempt to transfer the nitrogen-fixing ability of the latter to the former. Such an accomplishment, however, appears to be far in the future, if indeed, it is ever realized. Finding ways to introduce nitrogen-fixing microorganisms directly into the cereals appears more likely. A recent report of maize in Brazil growing in association with a nitrogen-fixing bacterium is most encouraging. Research is currently being devoted to determining if widespread use can be made of this discovery.

In the process of photosynthesis plants utilize carbon dioxide from the air to make food. Some plants, known as $C_4$ species, including maize, sugar cane, and sorghum, are more efficient than others, the $C_3$ species. There are hopes of making plants of the latter group more efficient in their use of carbon dioxide by some as-yet-undiscovered technique. It has also been suggested that it might be possible to improve the energy efficiency of crop plants, which use only about one percent of the sunlight that falls on them for photosynthesis. If plants could make greater use of the sun's energy we could expect higher yields than are presently secured.

How are these changes to be accomplished? Perhaps they can be achieved by some form of genetic engineering in which plants will be manipulated in new ways. It has been suggested that culturing of single cells or tissues of plants in the laboratory offers hope of going beyond the traditional techniques of breeding. Through cultivation of individual cells it may be possible to make hybrids between organisms that cannot be hybridized by ordinary techniques. At present the breeder can only make crosses between closely related species belonging to the same genus, and frequently it is not even possible to secure hybrids between these. It has also been suggested that it may be possible to obtain a more rapid multiplication of desirable plants by single-cell culture than by growing the plants from seed or using ordinary methods of vegetative propagation. Other possibilities offered by single-cell culture are the obtaining of disease-free plants and the obtaining of haploid plants from pollen. The latter would give plants that have half the number of chromosomes of the plant body, which could be most useful in some breeding programs.

Greater investment in basic research will be required to advance these efforts. Two kinds of research may be distinguished—pure, or basic, and applied. The study of photosynthesis simply to learn more about how it operates—and, of course, we already have many such studies—would qualify as basic research. Such studies do not necessarily have any immediate practical objective and may never have any practical application. They are vitally necessary, however, to furnish the information we need for any attempt to improve our food plants. Direct attempts at improving food plants, of course, would be applied research. There is sometimes greater difficulty in getting financial support for pure than for applied research, but without the basic knowledge furnished by the former, the latter type of research could not exist very long. Gregor Mendel did not set out to make a better pea when he began his hybridization of various varieties of peas. He was simply curious, and out of his curiosity came the laws of genetics, the basis of modern plant and animal breeding.

Clearly the breeders and other biologists can contribute further to the elimination of hunger and malnutrition in the world, but they alone can not be expected to solve the problem. The nature of the food problem and who is responsible for solving it will be discussed in the next chapter.

# 13

# Let them eat cake?

*It has been said, that the great question is now at issue, whether man shall henceforth start forwards with accelerated velocity toward illimitable, and hitherto unconceived improvement; or be condemned to a perpetual oscillation between happiness and misery, and after every effort remain at an still immeasurable distance from the wished for goal. . . .*

*I think I may fairly make two postula.*

*First, that food is necessary to the existence of man.*

*Secondly, that the passion between the sexes is necessary, and will remain nearly in its present state. . . .*

*Assuming, then, my postula is granted, I say, that the power of population is indefinitely greater than the power in the earth to produce subsistence for man.*

Thomas Robert Malthus, *An Essay on the Principle of Population, 1798*

The population of the world is now over four billion. How many of these people are hungry is difficult to determine, for there is no agreement on the definition of hunger, and moreover, exact numbers would be hard to come by. One recent estimate, however, has 500 million living on the verge of starvation and as many as one-third of the people of the world malnourished or undernourished. In the United States, people on the average obtain 3000 calories of food per day, and for the world as a whole the average is 2000 calories. In the poorest countries, however, the people average only 1000 calories a day; these are the hungry people of the world, and there are more of them than ever before in history.

It is generally agreed that enough food is being produced today so that no one in the world need go hungry. In fact, food production has more than kept up with the growth of population in the past few years, although the increased food production has been largely in the developed nations. The present food problem is not so much one of production as one of distribution. The distribution of food is controlled by a number of factors, the chief of which is money. Poverty is the greatest cause of hunger in the world. Even in the poorest nations, people with money do not go hungry.

Most current predictions indicate that the world's population will double in 30 years. The question to be asked is whether food production can keep up with the growth of population. The answer is far from certain. There are some who, with guarded optimism, believe that food production can keep pace with the increase in population, and others who feel that if we can drastically limit the growth of population there is hope. Still others, the "prophets of doom," think that it is already too late and that we shall have mass starvation before the end of the century.

Food production is in large part a biological matter. However, the food problem, as it may be called, is largely a social, economic, and political one, as has been repeatedly pointed out in the many books on the subject that have appeared in recent years. In this chapter attention will be focused first and primarily on the biological problems, but before doing so certain assumptions have to be stated.

First, we shall assume that there will be no serious long-term deterioration of the climate that could seriously affect food production. We may expect that floods and droughts will have adverse effects upon food production in small areas of the earth at any one time; but if there were an overall cooling or warming of the earth, agriculture would be drastically affected throughout the world. Some climatologists are predicting such drastic changes, but as yet there is no agreement as to the nature of the change or how soon it will occur.

For the purposes of the present discussion we shall also assume that enough energy will be available to support agriculture. The intensive agriculture that is the basis of the high productivity of the developed nations requires huge amounts of energy. The greatly increased yields in agriculture in the last 30 years have come about largely through high energy use. Under intensive agriculture 80 gallons of gasoline are required to produce 1 acre of corn, and 110 gallons of gasoline are required to produce food for one person for a year. In the United States, with abundant energy from petroleum, only two farmers are needed to produce food for 100 people, whereas in China over half the people must

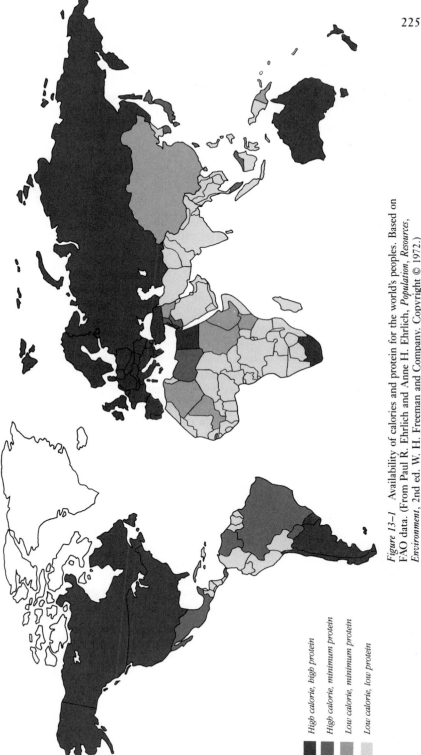

*Figure 13–1* Availability of calories and protein for the world's peoples. Based on FAO data. (From Paul R. Ehrlich and Anne H. Ehrlich, *Population, Resources, Environment*, 2nd ed. W. H. Freeman and Company. Copyright © 1972.)

High calorie, high protein

High calorie, minimum protein

Low calorie, minimum protein

Low calorie, low protein

work in agriculture to feed the country. It might be noted that the Chinese at present are attempting to increase the "efficiency" of their agriculture by replacing man power with other kinds of power. Some have long thought that important ways of improving agricultural productivity in the Third World would be greater mechanization and increased fertilization. One of the greatest impacts of the energy crisis upon agriculture has been in the increased cost of fertilizer. The large amount of petroleum necessary to produce fertilizer has put it beyond the reach of the poor farmer. Unless cheap alternative sources of energy are found soon, the prospect of greatly increasing agricultural productivity is remote.

Not too many years ago it was assumed that the oceans could supply more of the food for the world. The Russians and the Japanese in particular have depended heavily on the oceans for supplemental food. About 5 percent of the world's protein comes from the ocean at present, and some had predicted that the amount could be doubled or tripled. That, however, now appears most unlikely. Both over-fishing and pollution of the oceans have had deleterious effects on the yield in recent years. Moreover, distant ocean fishing, as opposed to coastal fishing, requires large amounts of energy. We may count upon the oceans to continue to supply some food, perhaps even more than at present with the greater use of fish that are now unpopular (the so-called trash fish) but we cannot assume that the oceans will contribute greatly to supplying the world's food needs.

From time to time articles have appeared in popular publications heralding some new discovery that would relieve the hunger problem. Among these have been the greater use of lower plants, the algae and the fungi. Certain algae and fungi, of course, have been used as food since the earliest times—seaweeds have long been used in the diet of Asian peoples, and mushrooms and truffles have been considered delicacies by nearly all people. These multicellular algae and fungi provide little in the way of either calories or protein. Some unicellular algae and fungi are good sources of protein, however, and the idea of using these microorganisms to manufacture protein for human consumption goes back a good many years. The algae, since they are photosynthetic organisms, can manufacture their own food from carbon dioxide using energy from the sun. In spite of all the publicity given to them, they have yet to contribute much. The procedures for growing them on a mass scale are not as simple as was once assumed. Moreover, the algae lack certain essential amino acids, and they are not easily digested unless the cell walls are first broken down. Their flavor is not acceptable to most people, but that, of course, could be masked in various ways.

Yeast, which can hardly be considered a new domesticated plant, is very efficient at converting carbohydrates into protein. As early as the Second World War, "meat" made partly from yeast was produced on an experimental basis. Yeasts, of course, are fungi and nonphotosynthetic, which means that they require carbohydrates and organic compounds as nutrients. Materials such as wood pulp, can, however, be used as a source of carbohydrates for their growth. Other microorganisms can also be used to produce protein, including some bacteria that give even higher yeilds than do yeasts. Some are being grown using a petroleum base as a food source. Considerable effort is now being made to use microorganisms to produce protein food, but some problems such as their purification for human use still remain. At present, single cell protein (SCP) as it is called, appears more promising as food for livestock than for humans, but such use should, theoretically at least, free more cereals and fish meal for human consumption.

Much of our packaged food from the grocery store or supermarket today contains various additives. For the most part these are used to improve the keeping properties and the appearance or flavor of the food. Although there has been criticism of many of the additives, some of it justified since they have been suspected of causing cancer, the modern life style of the industrialized nations calls for packaged food with a long shelf life. Some additives are also used for enrichment or fortification of the food. In many countries bread is enriched with thiamine, niacin, calcium, and iron. In some places thiamine is added to polished rice to prevent beriberi, or niacin to maize to prevent pellagra. These measures add certain essential nutrients, but do not compensate for the low quality of the protein of many plant foods, which could be improved by adding the amino acids lysine and methionine. The amount of protein in certain traditional foods could also be improved by adding proteins from other plant sources. In an attempt to improve the nutrition of the poor people of Central America, the Institute of Nutrition of Central America and Panama developed a vegetable flour, incaparina, made largely from cottonseed meal. Similar low-cost proteins from local products are now being made in other parts of the world.

One possible source of protein, largely neglected until recently, is the leaves of wild plants, of forest trees, for example, or of common weeds. The leaves of many domesticated plants are eaten, but these are hardly a major food source. Leaves, of course, contain protein, as we have already seen; in manioc, for example, they contain far more than the part traditionally eaten. They also contain a lot of indigestible fiber, and people could hardly eat enough of them to supply their protein needs, quite aside from the fact that they would find such a diet unattractive. For several years experimental work has been carried on utilizing leaves to supply protein to supplement ordinary foods. Although the possibilities seem enormous, so are the problems. It would be difficult to carry out such a program on a large scale in areas where more protein is most needed and also to gain acceptance of the resulting product as food. While we can expect greater use of various protein additives to our food in the future, they will not be a major contribution to the nutrition of many people for a long time to come.

Students sometimes ask why people don't domesticate new plants. As has been shown in earlier chapters, virtually all of the food plants were domesticated in prehistoric times; only a very few food plants have become cultivated recently. In North America, for example, cranberries, blueberries, and pecans, all of which were gathered by the Indians, have been domesticated in the last two centuries. No major food plant has been domesticated in historic times; we have simply been content to try to improve those plants our prehistoric ancestors handed down to us. There are without doubt wild plants in various parts of the world that could be domesticated for food, but it would involve tremendous cost and work to bring any of them to the level of productivity of a wheat, a corn, or a rice. Although today little attempt is being made to bring new wild plants into cultivation, some effort is being made to develop "new" food plants from long-neglected domesticated ones. One example is pigweed, (various species of *Amaranthus*), a pseudocereal and one of the most ancient food plants of Mexico and Peru. The seeds of pigweed have a higher lysine content than do the true cereals. Another plant that has recently drawn considerable attention is the winged bean (*Psophocarpus tetragonolobus*), an old cultivated plant of New Guinea. Nearly all parts of it can be eaten, and it has a protein content equal to that of the soybean.

From the foregoing account it should be apparent that neither the oceans, nor algae and fungi, nor protein from leaves, nor any new crop can solve the problem of food shortages. This should not be taken to mean, of course, that a search for new foods should not be continued, for food from any source can help. It appears, however, that the great bulk of our diet for the forseeable future will probably come from the traditional sources, such as wheat, rice, corn, and potatoes. Therefore, our major effort should concentrate on improving the yields of these and other plants. This can be done by increasing the land under cul-

*Figure 13–2*  Leaves and pods of the winged bean.

tivation and by increasing the yields of the land presently cultivated. Is this possible?

At present only about 10 percent of the world's land surface is under cultivation. About 17 percent is pasture or meadow, 28 percent is forested or woody areas, and about 45 percent cannot be used for agriculture because it is too steep, too rocky, too dry, too wet, or too cold. Some estimates suggest that it would be possible to increase the areas under cultivation to 20 percent, but this could hardly be done in the next 50 years, if ever. Bringing more land under cultivation is not a simple matter, and the fact is that nearly all the land best suited to growing crops is already under cultivation or is occupied by cities, airports, ball parks, graveyards, and the like. In the United States in a recent twenty year period an area equal to the state of Ohio was converted to urban use. In addition, it is estimated that in the United

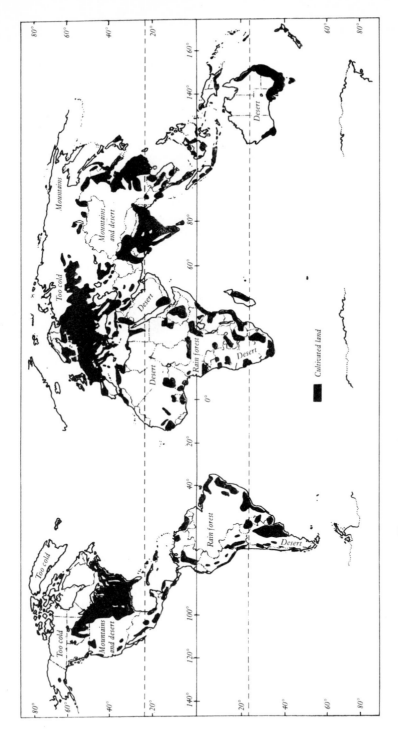

*Figure 13–3* Approximate area of cultivated lands of the world. (From Foreign Agricultural Service, USDA.)

States 3.6 billion metric tons of soil are lost to erosion every year. This means that land that is perhaps best described as submarginal for agriculture will have to be used, which will require great effort and great cost. Some of the recent attempts in Japan and the Soviet Union at bringing new land under cultivation have shown that the return is rather small.

Some of the pasture or grassland is not suited to growing crops, being at elevations too high for cultivated plants or in areas subject to severe erosion. Much of it, of course, now serves as grazing land for livestock and is thus already being used to produce human food. However, as we can feed about seven times as many people directly on plants as can be fed on meat, the question arises whether we should convert the pastureland to fields for cereals and legumes. As we have seen, citizens of the wealthy nations are the meat eaters, and there would certainly be considerable resistance to giving up meat. The problem is perhaps not so much that the animals need land—in fact, with modern animal-husbandry methods in the developed nations, farm animals are utilizing less land than formerly—but that at present the rich nations are feeding their animals plant and fish protein that itself could go a long way toward eliminating protein deficiency among humans.* As the population grows, the question of the reduction of livestock will have to be given serious consideration. A few years ago it was suggested that the first animals to go could be sheep that are raised for wool production. It was thought that plant and synthetic fibers could readily replace wool. Such replacement, however, does not appear as feasible as it once did, for synthetic fibers are made from petroleum. Our diet may be expected to be more vegetarian in the future than at present. However, though meat will be even more of a luxury than it is today, animals will still have the role of converting food that we cannot digest into highly digestible protein.

Still another way to obtain more land for the production of food would be to stop growing unessential plants now being cultivated. Tobacco immediately comes to mind. People could also learn to live without tea and coffee. Much of the land used for growing these crops is not, however, the best land for food plants. If, for example, tobacco were abandoned as a crop, it would create considerable unemployment and in that way might contribute to the hunger problem. This example

---

*On the positive side it should be pointed out that urea, a nonprotein form of nitrogen manufactured from inorganic compounds, is being increasingly used in the feeding of ruminants. One-third of their nitrogen can come from this source.

perhaps illustrates why the problem of hunger is so complicated. Drastic changes cannot be easily made without economic disruption. The day may come, however, when the luxury crops will have to be given up in favor of essential food crops.

A few years ago people looked to the day when the vast tropical forested areas would be used for food production. It is now thought that these tropical areas are probably best suited for growing what they have always grown—trees. When cleared, the land rapidly loses its fertility, and even with the addition of fertilizer little of it is suitable for sustained production of food crops. The advanced prehistoric cultures, with few exceptions, never developed in this kind of area, and then as now, the inhabitants of such areas depended on a slash-and-burn, shifting type of cultivation. Small areas are cleared and burned, crops are grown for a few years, and then the land is abandoned and a new area sought; obviously, this type of cultivation will not support a large population. In recent years Brazil has cleared vast areas of the Amazon region for modern agricultural development, and it is already becoming apparent that this may not be a wise development. It seems unlikely that we can count upon tropical forest areas to be a major contributor to the world's food supply.

Nor can we count on the timber areas of the temperate zones to contribute much in the way of food. Some forested areas are hardly suitable for cultivation, and it might be unwise to destroy the timber on those areas that could be used for growing food. For one thing, we desperately need the timber resources, and moreover, these forests are not in the areas where food is most needed. In China and some other places it is now realized that clearing forests was a mistake that resulted in severely adverse ecological consequences, and some areas once cleared are now being reforested.

Some land, too wet for conventional agriculture, might be drained to make additional land available for plants, but only at considerable expense; at the same time other land, too dry for agriculture, might be brought into cultivation with irrigation. We know, of course, from success in the southwestern United States and in Israel, for example, that such land can be made very productive, and many schemes are underway in various parts of the world to increase irrigation. The Aswan dam in Egypt was one such scheme, but unfortunately, by the time the dam was finished the population of Egypt had so grown that the country was in exactly the same situation as before the dam was built, as far as the need for food was concerned. Although we can count on some more desert land being brought into food production through irrigation, not all desert areas can be used. For one thing, there isn't enough water available. Although many people may think of water as cheap and unlimited, it is not. We will, in fact, face problems with water for our cities and our industries as the population grows. Sea water can be desalinated, but it will be too expensive to use on an extensive scale and we can hardly expect it to be widely employed for agricultural purposes, at least during this century.

Thus, if only a little additional land is going to become available for growing crops, we must make every attempt to increase the yields from the land presently being used. In addition to increasing overall yields, we should make more effort to increase the protein quality and quantity in the most basic food crops. Future breakthroughs in breeding by methods discussed in the last chapter are to be hoped for; however, no new development as spectactular as hybrid maize is visible on the horizon. At present, breeding efforts seem to be on a plateau, but when we realize that yields are three times as great in the developed nations as in the Third World, it is apparent that through application of our present knowledge much can be done to ease hunger in the world. The greater yields in the developed nations result partially from superior seeds, but largely from high energy use. Theoretically, at least, it should be possible to increase the yields in the Third World to equal those of the developed nations—if money and energy are available. We have only slowly learned, however, that increased yields in the tropics seldom result from simply transplanting the techniques used in other areas.

The Green Revolution is an example of what can be done. The new HYVs (high yielding varieties) created by incorporating genes for dwarfing and other desirable traits into wheat and rice, have had a profound effect on the yields of these crops, chiefly in Asia but also in some other parts of the Third World. Although some have considered the Green Revolution a failure because it did little to eliminate hunger, Nobel laureate Norman Borlaug, who was instrumental in the creation of the new varieties of wheat, has pointed out that it was not expected to solve hunger in the world, but would allow us to buy time to search for more permanent solutions. The potential contributions of the Green Revolution, however, were probably overemphasized. Yields seven times greater than those of the traditional varieties of wheat and rice were being claimed, when in reality the increases were nearer four times those of the traditional varieties, still a most significant achievement. The acreage planted to HYVs, some of which have recently been developed in participating countries, has increased steadily, but the yields have dropped considerably in recent years. There are two principal reasons for this decline: first, the best land was planted to the HYVs in the earlier years and less productive land is now being planted; and secondly, less fertilizer is now being used because its cost has increased with the advent of the energy crisis. It must be understood that the miracle seeds, as they have sometimes been called, are not alone responsible for the increased yields. The Green Revolution was a "package deal," requiring fertilizer, pesticides, and water for irrigation as well as superior seed. Several criticisms of the Green Revolution have been voiced. The most frequent one is that it has benefited the large farmers more than the small, poor farmers, which is true. There has also been concern that the mechanization and higher yields that accompanied the Green Revolution would contribute to rural unemployment by reducing the need for labor. It has probably done so in some places, but at the same time it has created employment in other places because the HYVs are more labor intensive. There was also concern that greater social tensions would develop, for those who participated in the Green Revolution would benefit greatly, thus creating a greater disparity between the "haves" and the "have-nots." There is as yet no clear indication that this has happened, but perhaps it is too early to be sure.

A potential danger of the Green Revolution arises from the fact that, as the HYVs replace the numerous traditional varieties, there is greater uniformity in the crops over wide areas. It thus becomes more likely that a disease might spread widely, destroying the crops more completely than was possible when there was greater diversity in the kinds of wheat and rice being grown. Finally, some have claimed that the Green Revolution is just another example of the transplanting abroad of American technology, and that the high energy demands of the Green Revolution are causing problems in many countries. While it is clear that another kind of revolution is still needed for the small farmers of the world, the Green Revolution does illustrate some of the things that can be done, as well as the sorts of problems that may be anticipated in planning future strategies for conquering hunger. Again it should be repeated that we still need large scale research efforts— both basic and applied.

Another possible way of increasing food production without finding new land would be through multiple cropping, that is by growing more than one crop a year. In many parts of the tropics it should be possible to farm around the calendar, and in some places today two crops of rice are produced on the same land in a given year. In parts of the midwestern United States a winter wheat crop is followed by soybeans.

More of this can be done, for presently much farm land lies idle even though the temperature is suitable for growing some crops. Intercropping, or growing several crops together, also deserves greater consideration. This is one of the oldest methods of agriculture—American Indians interplanted maize, beans, and squash—but today monoculture is the rule throughout most of the world. Intercropping, particularly for the small farmer, holds great promise and is already practiced on many small holdings.

If the loss from various pests could be eliminated, it would also make present crop land much more productive. It has been estimated that one-third to one-half of the crop in some regions, if not in the world as a whole, never reaches the consumer for whom it was intended, being lost to insects, birds, rats, fungi, and other organisms, even elephants. In one of his early books Lester Brown tells an amusing yet pathetic story. From various reports on the grain crop in India it was found that 50 percent was lost to rodents, 15 percent to cows, birds, and monkeys, 10 percent to insects, 15 percent in storage and transit, and 15 percent in milling and processing . Little wonder that India was hungry if 105 percent of the crop was lost! A slight exaggeration, of course, but it does emphasize not only the great need for better protection from pests, but also for better methods of harvesting, storage, and marketing of the crops in many countries.

The control of insect pests constitutes a major problem. Although the pollution caused by the use of chemical pesticides has been known for some time, huge amounts are still being applied on crops throughout the world. The chemicals used have many undesirable effects: People are exposed to toxic compounds that may be extremely harmful to them. A large number of organisms, including many beneficial ones, are killed along with the pests. Finally, the use of such pesticides leads to the development of resistance in the pest with the result that stronger concentrations of the pesticide or new pesticides are required. Some people maintain that without the extensive use of chemicals to control pests, it would be impossible to grow the large amounts of food now being produced. It should be clear, however, that we should strive to eliminate the use of these chemicals and adopt other measures to control the pests. Various means of biological control have been introduced with some successes. In many of these measures, natural enemies of the pest not harmful to the crop, frequently other insects, are employed to bring the pest under control. Such methods are hardly new, having been introduced in California in 1888 to control scale insects on citrus trees. At present, however, biological control is available for only a few pests of crop plants. A large amount of research and considerable money will be necessary before such measures can be widely adopted.

The problems are clear but the solutions are not. In recent years it has been popular to blame the developed countires for the plight of the poorer nations. Is it, then, the burden of the developed nations to put an end to hunger in the world? In 1974 Garrett Hardin published "Living on a Lifeboat." In his metaphor the world is an ocean in which there are lifeboats filled with the rich (the developed nations) and lifeboats filled with the poor (the developing nations). The latter are overcrowded, and as the poor people fall overboard they try to get on the lifeboats of the rich to take advantage of all of the "goodies" on board. Hardin assumes that the lifeboats of the rich hold 50 people and could safely take on ten more. If they take on all the swimmers, however, these lifeboats will sink. They could take on ten people and destroy the safety factor, but how does one decide which ten? Hardin feels that the solution would be to admit no people, or if one feels guilty about this he could jump overboard and let one of the poor people take his place. After discussing the reasons for his attitude, Hardin concludes that "for the foreseeable future survival demands that we govern our actions by the ethics of a lifeboat. Posterity will be ill-served if we do not." Thus one must ask himself if it is humane to save the lives of the poor people today if this means more deaths and suffering in the future. Needless to say, Hardin's article immediately brought about a number of editorials and articles in which the authors strongly disagreed with him. In fact, the word "obscene" has been used to describe his viewpoint. Whether people agree with him or not—and some do—his article certainly forced a number of people to think about the food problem.

One of the rebuttals in 1975 was by W. M. Murdock and Allen Oaten, colleagues of Hardin at the University of California at Santa Barbara. They start by asking whether the rich nations should continue to provide help to the poor ones, and their answer is a resounding "yes." They go on to point out that Hardin's metaphor is misleading: Lifeboats don't interact but nations do, for among other things the wealthy nations need materials from the poorer ones. With "considerable trepidation" they advance a foreign aid program for the United States that if "properly designed and properly used" could mean a considerable improvement in social wellbeing for the world. They propose that the United States should provide 10 billion dollars annually, which at that time was one percent of the Gross National Product or only 10 percent of the then current military spending. That sum would provide for family planning services, education to eliminate illiteracy, health care, a grain bank, fertilizer, and some help toward bringing more land under cultivation.

There is, of course, a big "if" in their program, for to do any good, as they admit, it would have to be properly designed and properly used. Two years earlier W. and E. Paddock brought out a book, *We Don't Know How*, in which they question whether the United States has ever carried out a foreign aid program that was effective. Others, too, have pointed out that our food aid has seldom reached the really hungry people.

So the question comes back to whether the United States should attempt to do anything about world hunger. Of course, those who believe that the United States should decrease or eliminate foreign aid programs designed for the poorer nations can use Hardin's and the Paddocks' arguments for support. This, however, is unlikely to represent the aims of a majority of people in the United States, most of whom presently like to think that through their government, their church, or their individual action they are doing something to help the poor and the hungry of the world. The United States has been generous in times of famine and other great disasters, but overall the financial contribution to relieve world hunger has not been great in proportion to its wealth. In fact, the United States ranks thirteenth in its share of monetary contributions toward fighting hunger; Sweden, the Netherlands, and Norway are among the leading contributors. These nations, of course, can afford to do more to try to eliminate world hunger, for they do not have the huge military complex that the United States maintains. Most of the foreign aid of the United States goes for military support.

In 1979 Robert S. McNamara, formerly the Secretary of Defense of the United States and now President of the World Bank, questioned whether the huge amount presently spent on the military does much toward promoting the national security that it is support to maintain. Pointing out that the amount now spent on arms research and development is more than "is spent on the problems of energy, health, education, and food combined," he maintains that poverty could be greatly alleviated by a "comparatively small contribution in money and skills from the developed world." Such a contribution, he claims, would not only help the security of the United States by helping to stabilize poor countries but also would assist the economy of the United States. If the question is put in these terms, perhaps more people in the United

States will be willing to see greater contributions from their country. Certainly we can not hope for much of a reduction in world hunger as long as the "great" nations are engaged in an arms race.

The elimination of hunger, however, is not just a problem for developed countries to deal with, for many of the poor countries could do far more than they are doing at present. Some of these countries have done little or nothing to attempt to control their population growth, and even though an effort is made to produce more food, food production cannot be expected to keep pace with unbridled production of people. The poor countries could also take other measures to relieve poverty. The income of over a billion people in the poorest countries averages around $150 a year. In some of these countries the income of the wealthiest one-fifth of the population averages twenty-five times that of the poorest one-fifth of the people. Although some countries have adopted land-reform programs that break up the large estates and distribute the land to the poor, much yet remains to be done. Graft and corruption are still a way of life in many of the developing nations. Mexico, for example, with its huge petroleum reserves, should be able to eliminate hunger, but will it?

Although the monetary contribution of the United States and other rich nations may be rather meager, many of these countries have played another role that is often greatly underrated. Through their research in birth control, in the breeding of plants and animals, and in the development of new agricultural techniques, they have made a major contribution to all the countries of the world. These countries have also played an important role in the education of students from the poorer nations. Although the criticism has been made that the students often receive courses of little value to them in their own countries, this is not always true. Another criticism, not the fault of the developed nations, is that far too often the students who receive their education there never return to their homes to put into practice what they have learned.

What will be the position of humankind in regard to hunger in the year 2000? Will there be wide-spread famine or even mass starvation, as some have predicted? Or will humanity have conquered the major problems of poverty, population, and food production, permitting all the people of the world to enjoy a high standard of living? No one really knows, but it seems likely that the situation will be little different from today. One-third of the world's people will probably still be malnourished, and this will involve far more people than it does today because of the increase in population.

# References

Anderson, Edgar, 1952. *Plants, Man and Life*. Little, Brown, Boston. (Written
for the interested layman; a rather unconventional but fascinating introduction to weeds, cultivated plants, and the botanists who study them.
Some of the material regarding the origin of certain crops has been
superseded by recent discoveries. Available as a paperback from the
University of California Press, Berkeley.)

Baker, H. G., 1978. *Plants and Civilization*, 3d ed. Wadsworth, Belmont, Calif.
(an abbreviated account of the most economically important plants.)

Chrispeels, M. J. and D. Sadana, 1977. *Plants, Food and People*, W. H. Freeman
and Company, San Francisco.

*Economic Botany*, the Journal of the Society for Economic Botany, published
by the New York Botanical Garden, Bronx, New York. A journal of
applied botany and plant utilization.

Harlan, J. R., 1975. *Crops and Man*. American Society of Agronomy, Madison,
Wisc. (A textbook dealing with the origin and evolution of crop plants by
an authority in the field.)

Hutchinson, Sir Joseph, ed., 1977. *The Early History of Agriculture*. Oxford
University Press, Oxford. (A collection of papers by specialists dealing
with the beginnings of agriculture and the origins of domesticated plants
and animals.)

Janick, Jules, Robert W. Schery, Frank W. Woods, and Vernon W. Ruttan,
1974. *Plant Science: An Introduction to World Crops*, 2nd ed. W. H. Freeman
and Company, San Francisco. (An introductory text covering botanical,
technological, and economic aspects of agriculture.)

Klein, Richard M., 1979. *The Green World: An Introduction to Plants and People*.
Harper & Row, New York. (An introductory textbook with interesting
historical accounts of economic plants.)

Purseglove, J. W., 1968–1972. *Tropical Crops: Dicotyledons*, 2 vols and *Tropical Crops: Monocotyledons*, 2 vols. Wiley, New York. (A treatment of virtually all tropical economic plants, many of which are also cultivated in the temperate zones. In addition to detailed descriptions and many illustrations, there are remarks on pollination, germination, propagation, chemical composition, husbandry, pests and diseases, breeding, and origins.)

Reed, C. A., ed., 1977. *Origins of Agriculture*. Mouton, The Hague. (Provides a variety of viewpoints concerning the origins of both plant and animal domestication as well as consideration of the early history of agriculture.)

Richardson, W. N. and Thomas Stubbs, 1978. *Plants, Agriculture and Human Society*. W. A. Benjamin, Menlo Park, Calif.

Riley, Carroll, L., J. Charles Kelley, Campbell W. Pennington, and Robert L. Rands, ed., 1971. *Man Across the Sea: Problems of Pre-Columbian Contacts*. University of Texas Press, Austin. (A series of papers dealing with many aspects of the controversy over diffusion versus independent invention. Papers are included on chickens, coconut, bottle gourd, sweet potato, maize, squash, and beans.)

Sauer, Carl O., 1969. *Seeds, Spades, Hearths, and Herds: The Domestication of Animals and Foodstuffs*, 2nd Ed. M. I. T. Press, Cambridge, Mass. (Much of this book is a reprint of the original edition published in 1952 under the title *Agricultural Origins and Dispersals* and hence does not take into account new information now available. Nevertheless, it remains one of the most stimulating discussions of the origin of agriculture.)

Schery, Robert W. 1972. *Plants for Man*, 2nd ed. Prentice-Hall, Englewood Cliffs, N. J. (An account of economically important plants, including those used for food as well as in other ways.)

Scientific American, 1976. *Food and Agriculture*. W. H. Freeman and Company, San Francisco. (Twelve articles by specialists dealing with food and the world's food problems.)

Seigler, D. S., ed., 1977. *Crop Resources*. Academic Press, New York. (Eighteen papers from the *Proceedings of the 17th Annual Meeting of the Society for Economic Botany*.)

Simmonds, N. W., ed., 1976. *Evolution of Crop Plants*. Longman, London. (An indispensable work for anyone interested in the origin and evolution of domesticated plants; cytotaxonomy, history, and prospects for all major crops, with notes on nearly all of the minor crops.)

Tippo, Oswald and W. L. Stern, 1977. *Humanistic Botany*. W. W. Norton, New York. (An elementary botany textbook with emphasis on economic plants. Excellent reading for anyone wanting to know more about plants.)

Ucko, Peter J., and G. W. Dimbleby, ed., 1969. *The Domestication and Exploitation of Plants and Animals*. Aldine, Chicago. (Original papers by fifty scientists dealing with virtually all aspects of domestication. Topics covered include the origin of domestication, methods of investigation, and human nutrition, as well as the treatment of many different plants and animals.)

CHAPTER 1

Braidwood, R. J., 1975. *Prehistoric Men*, 8th ed. Scott, Foresman and Co., Glenview, Ill.

Flannery, K. V., 1973. The origins of agriculture. *Annual Review of Anthropology* 2: 271–310.

Heiser, C. B., 1979. Origins of some cultivated New World plants. *Annual Review of Ecology and Systematics* 10: 309–326.

Redman, C. L., 1978. *The Rise of Civilization: From Early Farmers to Urban Society in the Ancient Near East*. W. H. Freeman and Company, San Francisco.

Renfrew, Jane M., 1973, *Palaeoethnobotany; The Prehistoric Food Plants of the Near East and Europe*. Methuen, London.

Sieveking, G., I. H. Longworth, and K. E. Wilson, eds., 1976. *Problems in Economic and Social Archaeology*. Duckworth, London.


CHAPTER 2

Allen, T. F. H., 1977. Neolithic urban primacy: the case against the invention of agriculture. *Journal of Theoretical Biology* 66: 169–180.

Cohen, M. N., 1977. *The Food Crisis in Prehistory: Overpopulation and the Origins of Agriculture*. Yale University Press, New Haven.

Dupre, Wilhelm, 1975. *Religion in Primitive Cultures*. Mouton, The Hague.

Eliade, Mircea, 1958. *Patterns in Comparative Religion*. Sheed and Ward, New York.

Gaster, T. H., ed., 1964. *Sir James Frazer's The New Golden Bough*. Mentor, New York. An abridged and somewhat revised edition of a classic work. Still probably the best source on myth, magic, and religion in relation to primitive and ancient agriculture.

Isaac, Erich, 1970. *Geography of Domestication*. Prentice-Hall, Englewood Cliffs, N. J.

James, E. O., 1959. *The Cult of the Mother-Goddess*. Praeger, New York.

James, E. O., 1962. *Sacrifice and Sacrament*. Barnes and Noble, New York.

Jensen, A. E., 1963. *Myth and Cult Among Primitive Peoples*. University of Chicago Press, Chicago.

Neiderberger, Christine, 1979. Early sedentary economy in the basin of Mexico. *Science* 203: 131–142.


CHAPTER 3

Caliendo, M. L., 1979. *Nutriton and the World Food Crisis*. Macmillan, New York.

Mayer, Jean, 1977. *A Diet for Living*. Pocket Books, Simon and Schuster, New York. (Answers to the layman's questions about nutrition by one of the foremost authorities on the subject.)

Pyke, Magnus, 1970. *Man and Food*. World University Library, McGraw-Hill, New York.

Simoons, F. J., 1978. Traditional use and avoidance of foods of animal origin: a culture historical view. *BioScience* 28: 178–184.

Smith, C. E., ed., 1973. *Man and His Foods: Studies in the Ethnobotany of Nutrition*. University of Alabama Press, University, Ala.


CHAPTER 4

Cole, H. H. and M. Ronning, ed., 1974. *Animal Agriculture: The Biology of Domestic Animals and Their Use by Man*. W. H. Freeman and Company, San Francisco.

Harris, Marvin, 1974. *Cows, Pigs, Wars & Witches: the Riddles of Culture*. Random House, New York.

Herre, Wolf and M. Röhrs, 1977. Zoological considerations on the origins of farming and domestication. In *Origins of Agriculture*, ed. C. A. Reed, pp. 245–279. Mouton, The Hague.

Smith, Page and C. Daniel, 1975. *The Chicken Book*. Little, Brown. Boston.

Zeuner, F. E., 1963. *A History of Domesticated Animals*. Hutchinson, London.


CHAPTER 5

Chang, T. T., 1976. The origin, evolution, cultivation, dissemination, and diversification of Asian and African rices. *Euphytica* 25: 425–441.

Doggett, H., 1970. *Sorghum*. Longman, London.

Grist, D. H., 1968. *Rice*, 5th ed. Longman, London.

Katz, S. H., M. L. Hediger, and L. A. Valleroy, 1974. Traditional maize processing in the New World. *Science* 184: 765–773.

Mangelsdorf, P. C., 1974. *Corn: its Origin, Evolution and Improvement*. Harvard University Press, Cambridge, Mass.

Quisenberry, K. S. and L. P. Reitz, eds., 1967. *Wheat and Wheat Improvement*. American Society of Agronomy, Madison, Wisc.

Sprague, G. F., ed., 1977. *Corn and Corn Improvement*, 2nd ed. American Society of Agronomy, Madison, Wisc.

Walden, D. B., ed., 1978. *Maize Breeding and Genetics*. Wiley, New York.


CHAPTER 6

Barnes, A. C., 1974. *The Sugar Cane*, 2nd ed. Wiley, New York.

Deerr, Nöel, 1949. *The History of Sugar*, 2 vols. Chapman and Hall, London.


CHAPTER 7

American Peanut Research and Education Association, Inc., 1973. *Peanuts— Culture and Uses*. Oklahoma State University, Stillwater.

Caldwell, B. E., ed., 1973. *Soybeans: Improvement, Production and Uses.* American Society of Agronomy, Madision, Wisc.

Food and Agricultural Organization of the United Nations, 1977. *Food Legume Crops: Improvement and Production.* FAO Plant Production and Protection Paper 9. Rome.

Milner, Max, ed., 1975. *Nutritional Improvement of Food Legumes.* Wiley, New York.

National Academy of Sciences, 1979. *Tropical Legumes: Resources for the Future.* Washington, D. C.

Norman, A. G., ed., 1978. *Soybean Physiology, Agronomy and Utilization.* Academic Press, New York.

Smartt, J., 1978. The evolution of pulse crops. *Economic Botany* 32: 185–198.

CHAPTER 8

Coursey, D. G., 1975. The origins and domestications of yams in Africa. In *Origins of African Plant Domestication*, ed. J. R. Harlan. pp. 383–408. Mouton, The Hague.

Dole, G. E. 1978. The use of manioc among the Kuikuru: some interpretations. In *The Nature and Status of Ethnobotany*, ed. R. I. Ford, pp. 217–247. Museum of Anthropology, University of Michigan, No. 67.

Hawkes, J. G., 1967. The history of the potato. *Journal of the Royal Horticultural Society* 92: 207–224, 249–262, 288–302.

Hawkes, J. G., 1979. Evolution and polyploidy in potato species. In *The Biology and Taxonomy of the Solanaceae*, ed. J. G. Hawkes, R. N. Lester, and A. D. Skelding. pp. 637–665. Academic Press, London.

Rogers, D. J. and S. G. Appan, 1973. *Manihot, Manihotoides* (Euphorbiaceae). *Flora Neotropica*, Monograph 13. Hafner, New York.

Simmonds, N. W., 1966. *Bananas*, 2nd ed. Longmans, London.

Yen, D. E., 1974. *The Sweet Potato and Oceania*. B. P. Bishop Museum, Honolulu.

CHAPTER 9

Child, Reginald, 1974. *Coconuts*, 2nd ed. Longman. London.

Harries, H. C., 1979. The evolution, dissemination and classification of *Cocos nucifera*. *Botanical Review* 44: 265–319.

CHAPTER 10

Carter, J. F., ed., 1978. *Sunflower Science and Technology*. American Society of Agronomy, Madison, Wisc.

Elliott, F. C., M. Hoover, and W. K. Porter, Jr., eds., 1968. *Advances in Production and Utilization of Cotton*. Iowa State University Press, Ames.

Heiser, C. B., 1976. *The Sunflower*. University of Oklahoma Press, Norman.

CHAPTER 11

Amerine, M. A. and V. L. Singleton, 1968. *Wine.* University of California Press, Berkeley.

Bailey, L. H., 1976. *Hortus Third, A Concise Dictionary of Plants Cultivated in the United States and Canada.* Macmillan, New York.

Fernald, M. L. and A. C. Kinsey, 1958. *Edible Wild Plants of Eastern North America* (rev. by R. C. Rollins). Harper, New York.

Heiser, C. B., 1969. *Nightshades, the Paradoxical Plants.* W. H. Freeman and Company, San Francisco.

Heiser, C. B., 1979. *The Gourd Book.* University of Oklahoma Press, Norman.

Janick, Jules and J. N. Moore, eds., 1975. *Advances in Fruit Breeding.* Purdue University, West Lafayette, Ind.

Rick, C. M., 1978. The tomato. *Scientific American*, August, pp. 76–87.

Rosengarten, Frederic, 1973. *The Book of Spices*, rev. ed. Pyramid Publications, New York.


CHAPTER 12

Carlson, P. S., 1975. Crop improvements through techniques of plant cell and tissue culture. *BioScience* 25: 747–749.

Frankel, O. H. and J. G. Hawkes, eds., 1975. *Crop Genetic Resources for Today and Tomorrow.* Cambridge University Press, Cambridge.

Scott, Tom K., ed., 1979. *Plant Regulation and World Agriculture.* Plenum, New York.

Stebbins, G. L., Jr., 1977. *Processes of Organic Evolution*, 3rd ed. Prentice-Hall, Englewood Cliffs, N. J.


CHAPTER 13

Abelson, Philip H., ed., 1975. *Food, Politics, Economics and Research.* American Association for the Advancement of Science, Washington.

Brown, Lester R. with Eric Eckholm, 1974. *By Bread Alone.* Praeger, New York.

Brown, Lester R., 1978. *The Twenty-Ninth Day: Accommodating Human Needs and Numbers to the Earth's Resources.* Norton, New York.

Eckholm, Erik, 1976. *Losing Ground: Environmental Stress and World Food Prospects.* Norton, New York.

Ehrlich, Paul R., A. H. Ehrlich, and J. P. Holden, 1977. *Ecoscience: Population, Resources, Environment.* W. H. Freeman and Company, San Francisco.

George, Susan, 1977. *How the Other Half Dies: The Real Reasons for World Hunger.* Allenheld, Asmun. Montclair, N. J.

Hardin, Garrett, 1974. Living on a lifeboat. *BioScience* 24: 561–568. (See also, E. M. Leeper, A chat with Garrett Hardin. *BioScience* 26: 785–787, 1976.)

Huddleston, Barbara and Jon McLin, eds., 1979. *Political Investments in Food Production.* Indiana University Press, Bloomington.

Janzen, D. H., 1975, Tropical agroecosystems, *Science* 182: 1212–1219.

Lappé, Frances M. and Joseph Collins with Cary Fowler, 1977. *Food First: Beyond the Myth of Scarcity.* Houghton Mifflin, Boston.

Lucas, G. R., Jr. and T. W. Ogletree, eds., 1976. *Lifeboat Ethics: The Moral Dilemmas of World Hunger.* Harper and Row, New York.

Murdock, W. M. and A. Oaten, 1975. Population and Food: Metaphors and the Reality. *BioScience* 25: 561–567.

Myrdal, Gunnar, 1971. *The Challenge of World Poverty.* Random House, New York.

Nicholson, Heather J. and R. L. Nicholson, 1978. *Distant Hunger: Agriculture, Food, and Human Values.* Purdue University, West Lafayette, Ind.

Paddock, William C. and E. Paddock, 1973. *We Don't Know How.* Iowa State University Press, Ames.

Pimental, David, William Dritschilo, John Krummel, and John Kutzman, 1975. Energy and land constraints in food protein production. *Science* 190: 754–761.

Scrimshaw, Nevin S. and Moisés Béhar, ed., 1976. *Nutrition and Agricultural Development: Significance and Potential for the Tropics.* Plenum, New York.

Simon, Arthur, 1975. *Bread for the World.* Paulist Press, Ransey, N. J.

Willett, Joseph, 1976. *The World Food Situation: Problems and Prospects to 1895,* 2 vols. Oceana, Dobbs Ferry, N. Y.

Wittwer, S. H. 1979. Future technological advances in agriculture and their impract on the regulatory environment. *BioScience* 29: 603–610.

Wortman, Sterling and R. W. Cummings, Jr., 1978. *To Feed this World: The Challenge and the Strategy.* Johns Hopkins University Press, Baltimore.

# *Index*